I Hear You...But What is God Saying?

Our Questions and the Answers We Must Receive from God

Apostle E. Uche Nyeche

authorHOUSE®

AuthorHouse™
1663 Liberty Drive
Bloomington, IN 47403
www.authorhouse.com
Phone: 1-800-839-8640

Published by AuthorHouse 04/11/2014

ISBN: 978-1-4969-0488-1 (sc)
ISBN: 978-1-4969-0490-4 (hc)
ISBN: 978-1-4969-0489-8 (e)

Library of Congress Control Number: 2014906957

The Author, Apostle E. Uche Nyeche, writes with conviction and unapologetically lays out some of the ills in our relationship with God and His church. Like Jeremiah, the author is fearless and bold in charging us to ask questions of God as He would welcome us to. Our purpose must be to hear from God not in error but in the clarifications of a deepened faith in Him in enablement of us to defend our faith in Truth and by Deed to His honor. As one who is *called* of God, for God, and with his rich knowledge of the Word, and his 'Spiritual well,' the enrichment in his writing is that of an anointed apostle. The breath of fresh air is the affluence both in philosophical thinking and the theologically exposition of his latest work.

~~~~~~

"A raw, authentic and timely work! Apostle Nyeche spares no expense in exposing what prevents God's chosen elect from surrendering all. He shares the hounds of Pride that continue to stand between Creator and Creature. A Sobering Read!"

-Pastor Candace Kelly, MDIV., Senior Pastor
Acts Community Bible Church

Dedication

I Hear You!...But What is God Saying? is dedicated to all those in the work of God who have been faithful to their *Calling,* also to the Soldiers of the Cross around the world who labored and died for their conviction towards Jesus Christ. It is with ultimate humility that I write to dedicate *I Hear You!...But What is God Saying?* to the forgotten memories of the early pillars of faith all over the world. It is through your work of labor that the foundation of our faith has stood; may your blessed memory forever be remembered. Amen.

Contents

Foreword

*"Rather, speaking the truth in love, we are to grow up in every way
into him who is the head, into Christ."* ~Ephesians 4:15

Everyone should have someone to speak truth into their life.
Throughout my life I have had the privilege of being blessed by the
wisdom of spoken truth from pastors, mentors, and friends. Truths
that in some situations have convicted me to personally evaluate my
walk with Christ, truths that warranted repentance, and on more than
one occasion, completely altered the direction of my ministry. Sadly,
many Christians don't have such a person to speak an edifying truth
into their life. Instead, they will seek out the latest self-help program
and in the process negate God's directing voice through Word and
Spirit. We rarely take the time to reflect to thank God for allowing
our lives to intertwine with the life of another, because we fail to
be aware of the movement of the Holy Spirit in the moment. Many
contemporary Christians seem to have forgotten the designation of
the Holy Spirit in the Triune Godhead. For many the Holy Spirit
is little more than an inclination, not the ever-present reality of the
Almighty God. The Holy Spirit lives and moves and has its being
among us, speaking to us, convicting us, guiding us, teaching us,
growing us.

When I first met the author many years ago at Fuller Theological
Seminary in Pasadena, California I had no inclination that our
relationship would continue beyond the confines of the classroom.
Nor did I imagine the blessing that his words of truth have been, and
I'm certain will continue to be in years to come. But I am eternally

grateful that it has. Throughout our personal and professional relationship he has shown himself to be a man after God's own heart, a servant to his Heavenly Father, and abidingly obedient to the Holy Spirit.

Beloved, God is still in the business of speaking to his people. Let us never forget, God speaks to his people through the Holy Spirit, we only need to listen. With his first book, *Because God Smiled, I am Laughing!,* Apostle E. Uche Nyeche boldly shared the convictions for God's church that had been laid upon his heart by the Holy Spirit. Perhaps it is only fitting that his second book is about that very topic-obedience to the Holy Spirit. My prayer for you, the reader, is that you are awakened by the words of wisdom encased in pages that follow. May you be blessed, challenged, and strengthened as you begin to look, listen, and respond to the work of the Holy Spirit.

Rev. Michael L. Woosley, Missio Dei Ministries
Sr. Pastor, Olive Branch Community Church, Bakersfield, CA
June 2013

Preface

I Hear You!...But What is God Saying? was written for all those who have wondered if it is alright to question God. For those who are walking with God in ministry, and also those who have a personal walk with the LORD but may be unsure of what they are hearing from God, this book is for you. This is a book I have written for all to know that God seeks and welcomes our interactions with Him when we search for a clear understanding of what it is that He is requiring of us. But we must be clear of what our intentions are before approaching God. If our aim is to avoid life mistakes that often are bound to derail our ability to walk in the providence of life, this is the book for you.

I do not assume that our honest desires to serve our God are in anyway clothed with the walk of disobedience rather the cloak should be in the desires of obedience to honor God because we love Him. To ask questions of God is to strengthen our faith and gain the assurance of who we are in Him. It is our having the knowledge that God is leading us and that the work we are embarked on is His, not ours. Most in generations before us never followed a path on doing His work without asking questions. They understood that it was the proper thing to do if they were to succeed in the work for which they are called for. We in our time have to understand that our work in the ministry can only be successful when in the leadership or the assignment we are given; we are led by none other but God through the Holy Spirit.

The goal for this book is to make clear that we are hearing from

God in any given situation. It is for us to have an understanding of what He is saying to us, and what God expects of us in situations regardless of the human wants or desires. This book informs that God welcomes our questions in moments of doubt and desires that we hear Him correctly so that honor and glory may be His. Much of the goal is focused on hearing from God and our ability to ask Him questions. There are those in faith who need to know that the attitude of our questions always should be centered on a heart of obedience to be in His blessings. God's grace, blessings, judgments and redemption have continued to this day, based on how we as His children are obedient to His commands. Therefore our purpose for the questions we ask God must be of good intention to receive whatever answer we get from the LORD, even when that answer is contradicting our original held beliefs.

My plan here is simple; to follow the examples of the biblically laid foundation before us of how the characters questioned God, and how God responded to them when they were obedient, with blessings. And also, to see how disappointing their journey was whenever they walked in disobedience. That which is set in our Christian tradition of the Holy Bible is what I have tried to bring to the forefront to exhort faithful believers on what is required of us. My other purpose here is to drive home a consistent method of mindset on what we can expect to see from the true life of a converted servant of God. Also to know what a Christian church should be which is to know that no matter what culture one is from we as Christians are *one* in Christ Jesus. I have made every effort in this book to be theological and yet more philosophical in thought in each chapter to spark the interest of the reader to engage more in the spiritual walk with God.

In order to serve the reader well I want to address my format of writing. My last book was a *book in a hurry;* it was like a baby that could not wait to come out of the mother's womb. I cannot explain why, but that was the feeling. This book I have written methodical and without that same rush I felt on the first one. Yet I know that as an imperfect human being regardless of our well intentions, mistakes somehow find their way but serious readers will not be distracted by minor grammatical or punctuation errors. Some of my mistakes may be the way I chose to phrase my thoughts. It is on this point I want to address that a phrase is a characteristic way or mode of expression. To some my style may be different but it does not diminish the message or reflect on ones level of intellect. There is not just one mode of expression, else all writing and speaking would grow dull. I plead to all those reading that my goal in writing is for the readership of the world-wide, not to a particular segment of the world population, but to all globally. With this in mind, I want to state that English expressions are not the only expressions used in this global world in which we live. I also think that each of us, no matter who we are, we write with distinctive characteristics and it is my goal in my writing to keep that character unique to my way.

I pray that as you read *I Hear You!...But What is God Saying?* that you will find it informative, which my goal is, and enjoyable at the same time.

Be blessed in the name of Our Lord Jesus Christ.

Introduction

I learned long ago that when the Holy Spirit directs someone to say or do a certain thing, first of all, it often manifests in an uncommon way that disturbs ones auto-pilot way of logical thinking and understanding. We look for some common thread to hold on to and when we do not find one, rather than seeking God's guidance and exercising our faith, we toss it aside because it is not familiar. This sort of cerebral thinking would have sent Apostle Paul of the Bible running the opposite direction when he heard a voice coming from heaven saying, "Saul, Saul, why are you persecuting me?" It was the voice of Jesus Christ. Those of you that have trouble believing that this actually occurred may also have trouble believing that God created the universe, and so you are struggling with the elementary concepts of God. But Apostle Paul's unique experience is one example that establishes the fact that it is the same Holy Spirit that dwells amongst us today who still manifests Himself in ways that we may not understand. In addition, when there is a supernatural event or occurrence, we can find the move of God in the life of that individual as supporting evidence that they are not merely walking in the flesh. With that said, my desire is to help those that might approach Apostle Uche's writing with less than an open spirit so they may turn to recognize that God has called him to this writing.

If you have decided to read this book to find out who Apostle Uche is and to examine his ways and thoughts, you have already missed the point of his writing. Apostle Uche is a vessel God uses to pour out His wisdom and love to those willing to receive. What you will find is a man surrendered to the will of God who wants nothing more than to love God's people. Just like the prophets Elijah and Elisha of the Bible, Apostle Uche aims to restore respect for God and His message. When we listen and obey God, He is able to perform miracles in our life but we must be willing to faithfully follow Him. More than anything else we must desire a relationship with God and learn what He expects of our daily lives. Because it can often be difficult to discern when we are hearing from God, we must prayerfully read the Word of God. Psalm 119:29 says, "Keep me from lying to myself; give me the privilege of knowing your law." Maybe you privately tell yourself that you do not want to ask God any questions, because if the truth be told, you don't want surrender and obey. If this is so, Satan has you right where he wants you to be.

It is through knowing the Word and submitting to the leading of the Holy Spirit that we can live a victorious life and grow in Christian maturity. For this reason, Apostle Uche desires to communicate to all, what the Lord has revealed to him through the Holy Spirit and by way of life experience and academia. His heart's desire is that you would approach this writing with a willing spirit to know more about the Lord Jesus Christ and be transformed by faith in your inner man. As Apostle Uche always says, "we are nothing and can do nothing without God." Find time each day to know Him in a deeper way and ask the questions that will bring you to a life of holiness. It is the most valuable thing you can do for yourself and those that you love.

By Deborah Nyeche

Special Thanks

Thanks to the Creator of Life, God Almighty who has given me the fortitude to write. There is no question that without Him I am nothing. My whole life as it exists is dependent upon His grace and to that my humble adoration is forever His.

My mother Eunice (Tata) Wobo Nyeche, you are a blessing and a great mother.

To my dear and beloved wife, Deborah Nyeche (The Lady), whose thoughts are invaluable to me, in moments of my writers block, your insight stabilizes me and stimulates my thoughts. You are an asset and truly the wife of Proverbs 19; I love you so much.

The children of God given to me, Uche Jr. and Adarundah Nyeche, I love both of you equally and completely. I pray God's Hands will forever be upon both of your lives for His glory. My stepchildren, it is my prayer that God will guide your paths in life.

To my nephews and nieces, some of you I have known and some because of distance we have yet to know each other; I love all of you.

My brothers, and sisters, uncles, cousins, aunts may God bless each one of you. Attorney Tony Molino, words alone will not be enough to express my gratitude to you; God keep you always.

I Hear You!...But What is God Saying? was finished almost a year ago but it sat in a folder waiting for the appointed time of public release. It took the generous gift of grace through God, to use his servants, Richard and Sharon Knox, for this hope of publication to be made possible.

Thank you, Richard and Sharon for allowing God to use you for His glory. May God bless you for your faith in Him and in believing who He is in my life.

I Hear You! But What is God Saying?

I Hear You*!...But what is God Saying* is a title that came after I thought I had already established a title. My focus was on something other, but I was grabbed by forces beyond me and I knew it had to be. "I Hear you!...*But what is God Saying*," is truly an expression of mine in response to a chapter in my life with someone who was not outside the bounds in their desire, but whose will was not surrendered to God. How I had wished that my own honest commitment to be submitted to the ways of God had been shared. If there is anything that I have stood for, it is the true effort by God's grace to be obedient to God. In the early years of my life I did lead my own path and have seen the mistakes of a mortal man and the weary brunt of those mistakes.

Some of the readers here might say what he is talking about. After all, mistakes are a part of life. Yes, if you say this you are right in some sense. I actually believe and do often state that the day we stop making mistakes in life is the day we as humans cease to live. I agree that the mistakes of life are not necessarily a failure, rather they are of places where we learn something new from what one never knew; and now knowing to do the right thing, by knowing what we did not know how to do. But, there are mistakes in life we may never have to make to begin with if we choose to listen, especially to God. Such mistakes are very costly and sometimes some of us don't come out of it. It was such that I could have easily made a mistake of a grave consequence if I followed the flesh.

There is a clear example of such costly mistakes in the Bible as a reminder for us if we are willing to listen. It was that of Sampson and Delilah in Judges 16. When we walk in disobedience there can be severe penalty and it is what I am writing about. The consequences of a half-hearted obedience to God will never go unseen by the omnipresent Holy God with His omnipotent power, and you are guaranteed to pay a price.

Years have gone by now and I often have wondered why it is that "what is not of God" we as people enmesh ourselves with? And how much of a better life would we have if God directed our paths? And why do we make bad choices instead of good choices? What is it that causes even the body of Christ, called Christians, to set themselves up in the embracement of disaster and shut God out? These are the questions that I try to answer in *I Hear You!...But What is God Saying?*, beginning with why as human beings we find it hard to follow God's path. Simply put, pride of depravity, it is one of the most debilitating chronic disease that humanity struggles with (it is an evil that engineers the destruction of humanity). Pride is the most incapacitating struggle for the entire human race. Another point is the prideful thinking that we are in control of our future which invariably means for us as people that tomorrow is guaranteed as is the rising of the sun.

The ethos responsible for the rejoinder that brought this title was an act based on the self-centered pride of life. Pride of life is very obstructive. Pride causes blockage of objective reasoning of truth. Pride does not listen, nor does it allow for the settlement of "no." Pride is the self-importance of "my way, or no way." Pride therefore causes us to lose our position in life and worst, it destroys a worthy life of peace and joy we are destined to have if not checked and remedied. Pride is indeed a destroyer of life.

Most cultures of the world teach that we are in control of our lives. I cannot write here to state how many times I have heard the president of this country, Barack Obama, make his speech with the famous phrase, "America is a place where if you work hard and play by the rules you can write your destiny." I have cringed every time he says that, because it is not the truth. But I believe that for some reason he believes what he says, which may be born out of his conviction, but is that really the case in America that everybody who works hard actually succeeds in writing their own destiny? There may be of course a small segment of the population whose hard work paid off, but equally to the truth is that many others worked hard and it never paid off. Some of these people may have been laid-off short of their retirement. For others the company went bankrupt. Some never made it due to relocation, some debilitating ailment due to work related environmental poison or work related injuries, or the bad investment by some of these companies left them holding an empty sack at the end. Various scenarios can be responsible for the outcome. To encourage people to work hard is one thing but when the rosy pictures painted become too rosy, they often wilt before our eyes.

While that may work for a political speech geared towards exciting the audience, the truth is that humanity is not in control and therefore we must learn to surrender ourselves to God. Our destinies are not in our hands else a great many would have written it differently. Is there a part of our life participation that God requires of us? The answer is yes, but not devoid of surrender. It is the surrender that causes us to walk in obedience and obedience motivates our walk of faith in God. For none amongst us knows what will happen the next minute, much more the next hour or day. How then can we be delusional in thinking that we are in control? A passage I referenced in my first book taken from the Bible, here again it says in Ecclesiastic 7:14, "In the day of prosperity be happy, but in the day of adversity consider- God has made the one as well as the other so that man will not discover anything that will be after him." We are to know that God alone knows the future and so He controls and withholds what is in it to come.

Sometimes we choose badly because we are confused of our purpose in life and to know is to choose rightly. Our ability to choose rightly can be achieved as we yield to God who knows what is in the best interest for us. Our question should not fall outside the realm of seeking God in relationship with Him as the guiding light for our lives. Another scripture that comes to mind as I write is (Psalm 119:105), "Your Word is a lamp to my feet and a light to my path." Gods Word is indeed a lamp that will direct our path if we are willing to allow Him in our lives.

The Word of God is the truth and that truth is God. Until we are willing to surrender our lives to God we cannot come to the knowledge of the truth. To the truly saved it is when pride is divorced, and obedience to the will of God is sought in life as the higher priority. My desire is to obey God; to do what is in His will for me in the aforementioned, which is what led me to the title of the book you are now reading - I Hear You!...*But What is God Saying*? How I pray that everyone reading this book will rise to ask the same question in whatever situation they may be confronted with. Trust and know that God's grace sustains His own; I am not in anyway saying that life's journey will be easy, but one thing I know is that the hand of God is wide and large enough to carry you through any adversity with peace, and in joy.

I must add that to choose to follow and hear God instead of following your own carnal desires or the alluring temptations of humanity, which is the "I Hear You!...*But What is God Saying*" title and message of this book, can also be hard and lonely but trust and know that at the end, with God you have victory. I say this because Romans 8 assures and informs us that when God is with you, there is nothing a mortal being can do to you. Stand firm, even if the majority have doubted your position and joined even in the chorus of your detractors; know that in the end they will join to celebrate you. God never fails in making your enemies your footstool. This is where self-declared enemies are put under your control; it is His promise to the righteous at heart and a guarantee indeed to those who are steadfast in their walk with the LORD. He does it just in that manner for His glory if we do not faint along the way. I pray that the truth will grip the unholy throat of evil and unleash courage into the hands of the righteous ones seeking to please Him; Amen.

Chapter 2

Why We Must Ask the Question

Asking the question becomes an act that is imperative if one desires to honor God and be in His will. To be presumptuous with God is to *Miss the Mark* and that does not glorify God and it is very dangerous in itself. The other reason for asking questions is that of faith and assurance of instructions we may have received; what do I mean? That you now know your hope is in the hand of a higher being other than yourself, this assures confidence and a fearless plan on the battle front. I am writing here out of my own practical life experience and application and seek to write in the next chapter, examples of those gone before us who asked the questions of clarity from God.

I have made the decision in my personal life and the ministry corporately that I will in no-way take a step not ordered by God. My whole aspiration is to do the will of God and devotionally I petition Him to lead me in all that I seek and ask of Him. I also pray God never to allow me to fall into the hands of those who will draw me further away from Him or violate His precepts; many of whom we may not have to travel too far to find because they are within the church. Why my prayers? I must pray so that the forces of the wicked may be defeated at all times and because the devil is real and seeks to devour the servants of God. We should at all times know that to leave one unguarded is to leave oneself vulnerable and available as a tool of the evil one.

Maybe in your mind you might be asking the question, is it necessary every time to pray to God before we embark on a life routine? The answer to your question is please, yes, and always. Why? Because Philippians 4:6 instructs us with this, "Be anxious for nothing, but in everything by prayer and supplication with thanksgiving let your requests be made known to God." I thought that God has given us all the power? True, but that power works through the spirit of man which is imperfect but the greater power is that of the Spirit (which is of the Holy Spirit) which is used and available when ones relationship with God is attuned and in His time. As human beings our power is as good as we are which means that we are limited in every way, and we are people without knowledge of what will be in any moment ahead of us. Someone might say well, I do not like my job; I prayed and God did not answer, so how do I know what He is saying? Good question, but we are commanded to keep praying or knocking, and in moments of silence from God it is time to be still and wait, which is why you are advised to keep praying or knocking to begin with. This is the order of the Lord in Matthew 7:7 that we are to Ask, Seek, and Knock, that everyone who does so will reap the benefit of obedience in doing exactly as He has commanded us to. But look closely at what the operative word in the teaching is, "will," which means in the future. There is no time table that is given rather we are to be rest-assured because we have continued in petitioning through praying to God and at His time will the answer come to us.

In my previous book I laid out such examples but in *I Hear You!...But What is God Saying?* I want to be specific in writing that to represent God and His kingdom is to do our best to avoid error as individuals. I write to those who are serious about their walk with God. God is always patient with us because He is patience. Our error therefore happens sometimes in our own impatience. We should ask questions to get God's direction and when we do, there are less chances of walking in falsehood or running the risk of chastisement from God. Except if we are seeking answers from God through sources that are not of God, and if that is the case, God will allow us to have such answers from those unlikely spirits. We have such examples of God at work and one can be found in the story of Ahab and his 400 prophets who were not true prophets of God (1 Kings 22:28). These prophets gave false prophecy of a victory in a war (1Kings 22:6b), "Shall I go against Ramoth-gillead to battle or shall I go refrain?" And they said, "Go up, for the LORD will give it into the hand of the king."

The prophets in 1 Kings worshiped the golden-calf at Bethel set up by Jeroboam (1 Kings 12:28). Ahab who supported this religious worship also worshiped Baal. His desire to receive favorable messages to go to a war he was not supposed to go to with victory was prophesied by his prophets. They spoke words that were designed to please Ahab and so the authoritative words of God were rejected. Micaiah in 1 Kings 22:15 sarcastically repeated the words of the message from the false prophets, "Go up and succeed, and the LORD will give it into the hand of the king," Ahab aware of the sarcasm demanded the truth from Macaiah in v.16. But Micaiah prophesied to him that the war was not for him to be won. The king was not pleased and complained that the prophecy towards him from Micaiah was always of evil and not of good. And then the unique work of God is revealed in v.20-23, The LORD said, "who will entice Ahab to go up and fall at Ramoth-gilead?" And one said this while another said that. Then a spirit came forward and stood before the LORD and said, 'I will entice him.' The LORD said to him, 'How?' And he said, 'I will go out and be a deceiving spirit in the mouth of all his prophets.' Then He said, 'You are to entice and also prevail. Go and do so.' Now therefore, behold, the LORD has put a deceiving spirit in the mouth of all these your prophets; and the LORD has proclaimed disaster against you." This reveals that in our asking questions our hearts must be sincere else when we are perverse and impure with God, God will be perverse and impure with us (2 Samuel 22:27). In 1Samuel 23:10, 30:7, 2 Samuel 2:1, King David in these chapters asked questions of God and had victories because God was leading him. Without God clearing the threat on his path David would have fallen into the hands of Saul, or even not had the victories that were before him.

Many times I have been saved from danger at the hands of

7

humanity with their disguises by listening to God and in turn being willing to accept the answer He gave to me. In such instances God will bring you through if you are willing to ask questions and wait for Him, at His time, for an answer before you proceed with decisions. Here are some examples from my experience.

Years ago a few members of our church made the decision while I was on a trip overseas, that moving the church to a different city location was the proper thing for the church without consulting God, nor myself as the shepherd of the house. Upon my return a source within the church revealed to me of what their intentions were. Without confronting them I waited for their expected presentation which was made known to me. My humble answer was to ask if I could seek the face of God for clarification. Gracious as they were, God in a week or two made it clear to me with these words, "tell them no, I called you, not them."

Our God answers prayers and Our God speaks clearly. On a personal level, my wife and I, in an effort to combine our home as one physical dwelling place both gave notice of our intentions to vacate from our current place of residence to a new location of spaciousness. But deep within I was troubled and concerned of the cost involved and I recall stating to my wife that I had reservations and informed her of my intentions to seek an answer from God. I recall her agreeing, knowing who I am with the Lord, and in her respect and love for the God we serve she agreed. Days would go by, when the Lord said to me with an audible voice, "it is not yet the time for you to move." This message I delivered to my beloved wife who simply agreed. We had so much that could not fit in a two bedroom, but there was a choice to be made and that choice was for us to listen to the instructions of God or follow our own way. Hard as it was, the rest of our belongings found their way into the storage for over two years because we chose the way of the LORD. Looking back now, God knew what was better for us. This is the choice we hear expressed all the time in ministry or teaching in the church that God has given us a mind to make choices but those choices cannot happen with God in absence. It must happen in His inclusiveness.

Moving some of our belongings to the storage was expensive but not what it would have cost us if we carelessly obligated ourselves to a costly commitment that we were not yet ready for. The great blessing here was that God knew all along what was best for us. It is essential to ask God questions. What we desire and want may be one thing, but what God is saying about the situation you may be about to embark on, is totally a different thing. Many of us Christians will find ourselves at peace and save ourselves from a heart ache if we are willing to allow God to guide us. God guiding you comes with your heart of honesty to yourself, and with intentions that are pure. Too often, too many of us called Christians, lie to their own detriment as if they can deceive God. Deciding not to go to church the night before and having a headache in the morning is not a confirmation that God is telling you *not to go to church.* We may use the situation as an excuse and claim that it is God, but have you just granted your own wish not to go to church? Choosing not to give your friend, sister, or brother a helping hand when the ability for you to do so is within, and somebody else shows up because you dragged your feet to rise to the occasion, is not the will of God, and God is not pleased when most of us so called Christians choose to be disobedient to God's commandment. So that we might be clear, Proverbs 3:27-28 states, "Do not withhold good from those to whom it is due, when it is in your power to do it. Do not say to your neighbor, Go, and come back and tomorrow I will give it, when you have it with you."

The Bible commands that when the need is there and the wherewithal is there you meet the need without any self-centered excuses. Asking the question for someone who calls themselves a Christian whether they should do something that God has already commanded through His Word, is to make a mockery of yourselves and your faith. When you are asked to sow a hurtful seed as a thanksgiving offering because God has blessed you and you struggle with it, choosing rebelliousness by reasoning your way out of adherence instead of obedience, know that God is not pleased. Looking around for an answer to the trouble you are now dealing with when you already know the consequences of the hell you now find yourself, is just your disobedience raining down suffering upon you and should be nothing to be blamed on God.

The question here speaks of what to do when the path is unclear and the directions unknown. You must advance in prayer, sometimes fasting, and wisdom. Never be afraid to consult with trusted spiritual leaders in your church. A matured Christian who has a praying life and is in relationship with God should take seriously the scripture in (Hebrews 11:6), "And without faith it is impossible to please Him, for he who comes to God must believe that He is and that He is a rewarder of those who seek Him." To seek God is to be willing to align ourselves according to His own will for our purpose. So many people and Christians alike do not want to ask questions and the reason why they do not ask relevant questions is because they have not prepared themselves to hear/receive when the answer may be "no," nor are they willing to accept the will of God for their lives. To ask questions is to yield to a higher power and authority who knows what is best. The will of God is in most cases, if not always, in direct conflict and in confrontation with our ego. A true Christian willing to serve God with the heart of obedience, will at all times seek to hear from God before they proceed with any action, whether it is marriage, purchasing of a building, assignment, acceptance or any movement at all. At times those answers may not be audible but surely if God is in it there will be symbolic signs from the LORD, because God speaks even more so in symbols.

The majority of those in the historical Biblical foundation chose to hear from God making sure that their path was led of God and this has always been from the beginning the method of operation, and is the foundation of the Christian movement. Shamefully there are too many performers of our time who dare not ask questions but through their worldly contacts and connections they assign to themselves things and call it God. Churches in our time struggle in areas of spiritual power because so many of the so-called leaders are not seeking the direction of God for the victory that may have already been ordained. Such work of the flesh does not and cannot please God, but it will please humanity since it is the work of flesh.

God will not inhabit the pride of humanity whose main goal is the glorification of the flesh. Grant it, that there are some who create the impressionable atmosphere of a true church with mimic of the power of God, but in the end only the sheep that follow blindly without asking questions are fooled. Asking questions whether in our relationship with God, with others, and by the members of the body called church, is to have a clear understanding. The consequences of not hearing from God or being led by Him can be a great tragedy.

This brings me to a chapter in Genesis where Abram failed to ask questions and did not listen to God. He listened to and was led by his wife without God directing him. God promised Abram an heir but there was no time-table as to when. Sarai being in her old age had not given him a child. But the Bible reveals the tragedy in the time of Abram and it is that of impatience for Abram and Sarai. Neither thought it could happen with them being late in their life. The story in the first chapter was that Sarai had bore him no children and so, the suggestion of a maid substitute by Sarai to Abram became the human answer to God's promise. In Genesis 16:2 "Sarai said to Abram, now behold, the Lord has prevented me from bearing children. Please go into my maid; perhaps I will obtain children through her." Now, the gravest mistake of not asking questions by Abram of God at that time is what has led to the turmoil between Israel and Palestine that the world is scratching its head over in our time not knowing how to find resolution. It was a mistake that could have been avoided. Why we must ask questions becomes highly important for us because in every situation it is essential, and there are always consequences when we do not wait on God. By waiting on God's direction and accepting that He knows best for you, will cause you to gain a deeper assurance of faith. He therefore expects us to ask questions in the areas of uncertainty. It will please God that His chosen honors Him in that manner of trust.

None other than the troubles we are bound to encounter, and the reverent fear of God, should help us see clearly the reason why we must be asking questions. The story of "The Golden Calf" in the Bible tells of Aaron the brother of Moses, who was supposed to lead the people in the absence of Moses who was up on the mountain. The people had grown impatient as often is the case of a visionless group or faithless church. Moses' absence was to them a sign of no God. A physical identifiable object (idol) had a meaning, probably because they were used to such in Egypt where they left from. So the next step for them was to build themselves a god and Aaron became their source of direction. This is what Aaron did when he was confronted by the people, it states in Exodus 32:1-2, "Now when the people saw that Moses delayed to come down from the mountain, the people assembled about Aaron and said to him, "come; make us a god who will go before us, for this Moses, the man who brought us up from the land of Egypt, we do not know what has come of him." Aaron said to them, "Take off the gold rings which are in the ears of your wives, your sons, and your daughters, and bring them to me." The Bible tells us that out of these Aaron without consulting God built a molten calf and said to them, this is your god.

This was a blunder on the part of Aaron as he did not seek God and did not have the conviction of inner strength to say "no" to the demanding public against their request from him. He could have told them that it was not a fulfillment he could make on his own but for them to wait on Moses or God. Instead this reveals something more about Aaron, that he was not cognizant of his limits or maybe there was low self-esteem on his part in the need to please, making him appear more caring of a person than his younger brother Moses. It also may be that he was afraid of the people and yielding to the pressure was the option left for him. Whichever it was, it speaks of the man Aaron. This is a character flaw that is not hard to find in some of our churches where people weak in leadership are bullied to acquiesce to demands that are contrary to the Word of God. This need to have pseudo peace does not help; neither does it create true peace and holiness. It is nothing but a slippery-slope to the entire body.

I am reminded of another story where a young unwed mother, a member of the church choir, got pregnant and the church pastor asked her to step aside. The grand-mother in her blindness to holy living saw nothing wrong and demanded her re-instatement or she was to see to it that the pastor was relieved of his position. Afraid of loosing his position the pastor relented choosing to offend God by pleasing the flesh.

From the story of the Israelites in the Bible we learn that the anger of God burned so much so that He decided to destroy the children of Israel. Except for the beseeching of Moses to God, they would have been wiped-out. The tragedy not to seek God's face or ask questions is costly, catastrophic, and sometimes deadly. At all times children of God must ask questions to avoid costly mistakes so that we will be on the side of God and in His will. Our journey therefore becomes a journey that not only will last but one of a successful race for the glory of the Lord Almighty.

May we at all times in obedience be led to learn to ask questions.

Chapter 3

Some of Those Before Us Who Asked Questions

When we are unsure of the assignment, our position should be asking question to avoid errors of service in operation and in judgment. All through the Bible questions were asked of God for clarification even in places of His promises. Starting with Abram when God told him not to fear and assured him a reward, Abram asked God what that reward was to be. Abram said, in Genesis 15:2, "O Lord God, what will You give me, since I am childless, and the heir of my house is Eliezer of Damascus?" Now notice that God answered Abram with a favorable answer to his question clarifying for him with assurance that his fears of a non-biological child being his heir was not part of His plan for his life. Did God stop with His words? Not really. God, as stated in the Bible took Abram out and showed him the stars of heavens as a symbol of his descendants that were to come. Saints of God, when in doubt we must ask questions especially those in leadership and positions of authority who administer and speak on behalf of God.

Asking questions, which God welcomes, however does not in any way mean we will receive a positive answer favorable to our position. Nevertheless we continue to see this formula all through the Bible which most of us in this day fail to read, nevertheless to follow. Abraham's name was changed from Abram. Now, Abraham said to God, in Genesis 17:18 & 19, "Oh that Ishmael might live before you!" but God said, "No, But Sarah your wife will bear you a son, and you shall call his name Isaac, and I will establish My covenant for his descendants after him." God here chose to do what he chose to do for His own glory, but at least the question was asked for clarification. I could write on the interactions and counter interactions of God and Abraham but I have chosen to bring others examples of those before us who asked questions.

The Mission of Moses in Exodus allows us to see another example of how those before us asked questions. And the success they had in their mission often was dependant upon the clarification of those questions for their assignment. The knowledge on their part was the assurance that God was the one leading them in their journey. In Exodus 3:1 Moses was called by God and there was an interaction and encounter between God and Moses in the bramble bush. The mission to go to Pharaoh was daunting for Moses and rightly so; he felt that this powerful King was not going to recognize him nor did he, a powerless man, think he was able to deliver his people from the hand of Pharaoh. Moses asked God the question in Exodus 3:11, "Who am I that I should go to Pharaoh, and that I should bring the sons of Israel out of Egypt." The answer that we get from God to Moses was a divine promise that He would be with Moses. This leaves no doubt of who is in charge of the battle and is an example to be used in the church of God today. It is the assurance of the leader going with convictions and fearlessness knowing that even when faithless people do not see how the battle can be won and they choose to make a mockery of the assignment, victory is on the way and those who mock will be proven wrong. Chapter 4 of Exodus is the place that I refer to as the battle of supremacy. God instructed Moses what to do and say in the rest of chapter 3 with the people in the communities of Canaanites and also the Egyptians but Moses' feelings of inadequacy needed the power of conviction, and so he asked. In Exodus 4:1 he states, "What if they will not believe me or listen to what I say? For they may say, The Lord has not appeared to you." The Lord returns the question with a question in answer to him by giving Moses enabling power as he handed him a staff and asked him what was in his hand. God commanded Moses to throw the staff on the ground which became a serpent; this threw Moses into a panic moment causing him to flee. God told Moses to take hold of the serpent. The Bible tells us that he grabbed the tail of it and the serpent turned to a staff. These acts were so that Moses and his people may believe that God was with them and was able as the same God of the patriarchs Abraham, Isaac, and of Jacob to bring him through.

Other miracles of God followed with God commanding Moses to put his hand inside his bosom which turned leprous as he took it out; only for it to return to its place of normalcy as he placed it back into himself. All these signs and many more of God's wonders with Moses served the purpose of assurance and conviction that indeed the Jehovah Yahweh was with him. Moses' questions cleared the air of uncertainty, fear, and doubt and established for Moses boldness and conviction. As Moses allowed God to lead, victory followed. All through as Moses walked with God, success for him and his people followed with their path led by God. Failures and disappointment engulfed or enveloped their path when they moved without God's direction.

As we continue with the events in the Bible there are many more others who asked questions. Isaiah in chapter 6:11, "Then I said," Lord, how long?" And He answered, until cities are devastated and without inhabitant, houses are without people and the land utterly desolate," How about Jeremiah? He said in Jeremiah 1:6, "I do not know how to speak, because I am a youth." God in this instance clarified for him the reason why his youth made no difference because the Lord was at work in his life. God's power is greater than our weakness. This became the fire that burned in Jeremiah throughout his ministry of fearlessness. And it is the fire that burns in the life of every believer who is assured of their calling from the Lord. The only time when there is no burning fire in the life of one who claims to be called of God, is when they are lukewarm or backsliding, or the claim of the calling a lie.

One of the most dramatic questions of encounter and interactions for clarification was that with Gideon and God in the book of Judges. Some expositions seem to suggest that the reason for these was Gideon's lack of faith; I do not know whether that is totally accurate.

In so many instances the expressed fear of death by Gideon may be his realization of his own inadequacy before this Holy God, and yet not understanding the reason why the God of his people who lead them through the Red Sea could not deliver his people from the Midianites. There is in this scene the sign of the fleece in Judges 6:36, "If you will deliver Israel through me, as You have spoken, I will put a fleece of wool on the threshing floor. If there is dew on the fleece only, and it is dry on all the ground, then I will know that You have spoken." Gideon, here was not in doubt of God whether He was with him; for he knew that God had already taken possession of him. For Gideon his calling was certain which was the assignment for him to deliver God's people. He was looking for certainty from God of His confirmation and assurance of God's presence to enable his accomplishment of the mission. In my personal life, I have no doubt of my calling and who I am in the Lord, and my realization that I am nothing without the enabling power of the Lord, is real. Any Christian who pride fully rejects this is delusional at best.

In the gospels we read the same examples of questions that took place with Jesus and John the Baptist, in Matthew 3:4, "But John tried to prevent Him, saying, "I have need to be baptized by You, and do You come to me?" This is the pattern that continued through out the rest of the Bible. It demonstrates for people that the order of spiritual things will not always follow human logic.

A question among many others is the event that occurred in the Damascus Road with Saul's conversion in Acts 9:4b, "Saul, Saul, why are you persecuting me?" Jesus asked. Saul answered (v5), "Who are You, Lord?" Jesus replied, "I am Jesus whom you are persecuting, but get up and enter the city, and it will be told you what you must do." Saul made certain whose voice he was hearing even though some might claim he already knew that it was the Lord. Jesus on the other hand made it explicit for Saul that there is an instruction that awaits him in the city as to what he must do.

Acts 9:10 is the encounter of God and His devoted servant called Ananias. Acts 9: 11 reads, "And the Lord said to him, "Get up and go to the street called Straight, and inquire at the house of Judas for a man from Tarsus named Saul, for he is praying, and he has seen in a vision a man named Ananias come in and lay his hands on him, so that he might regain his sight." What we read next in the chapter is the same classic example of what has been from Genesis, with Abraham and God. The scriptures state that in humble adoration to God, Ananias answered in Acts 9:13-14, "Lord, I have heard from many about this man how much harm he did to Your saints at Jerusalem; and here he has authority from the chief priest to bind all who call on Your name." Now, some might say that there are other motives why these questions and they may even draw a parallel to Jonah and his thought of Nineveh's undeserving redemption but Jonah and his case was a pure act of disobedience. Ananias, here was fearful of what he had heard about this man called Saul, and any of us in our day will be just as concerned. But I would think that his concern was that of the uncertainty of the man's character, whether there could be a true transformation in the life of Saul.

And so, in my own life when God speaks or instances where the inaudible push of the Spirit consumes me, I am constantly and repeatedly asking for the confirmation from God, whether He is the one leading me. God has never failed many ways to make Himself clear and in the accomplishment of His purpose for His glory.

Always know and be assured of who is leading in the journey.

Chapter 4

The Purpose Behind the Questions

The purpose for the questions must be understood by the saints of God that the questions asked must be asked for clearness. It is a question not only limited to our relationship with God but with others; meaning God, us and others. It is to honor Him as we walk with a surrendered heart in line according to His purpose; it is the outcome of our walk of love for all glory belongs to God. In the previous chapter I mentioned Gideon and God's encounter. God asked him to reduce the number of his foot soldiers. Why? That Gideon may not begin to ascribe to himself pride and arrogance. Deuteronomy 8:17 warns us of the dangers of pride where we begin to think that our own strength and power is all there is. It informs us to be aware that victories and successes are of God in all forms within our lives. It is to show that our character should be like of the one who called us, and to remind us that our blessings are of God. We are to walk in humility with regard to whatever we have. We should remain in the mood of giving glory to God and blessing those around us. Blessings of the Lord come with peace of mind, it is not puffed-up. I mentioned about the blessings of God in my last book and advised that Satan is in the blessing business too. When a gift comes through adultery it is not a blessing of God; when out of fornication you turn yourself to a cheap piece of meat for the purpose of receiving money/gifts, that is not the blessing that honors God. When one cheats another and gains materially, it is not of God.

When deceit conceived in the heart leads to a marriage, or any form of relationship, that, my brothers and sisters has nothing to do with God. God is pure and anything that is impure has nothing to do with God. But I write to state that God does not, and will not be found in an unholy act. To not know the purpose behind asking a question is to walk in disobedience with God. Yet we find that even in the Christian faith there are those who are quick to claim God as part in their sinful and illegally obtained material possessions, when Satan is their chaperon and has duped them. Satan will set you to fall into his hands against the laws of God, and then he locks you up in his prison yard of restlessness where the desire to belong and compete become a preoccupation. I have seen so many persons who named and claimed it in the name of the Lord, only to be destroyed. This is not namely directed to the unsaved (though they also are found guilty) but I am writing about those who may have spent 20-30 years in the ministry or church. These are people with high levels of education with titles, and well-known around the globe. They no longer seek God's face or listen to those who bring them warning from the Lord. In their worldly high-mindedness and intellectual self-aggrandizement they are now left spiritually blind and deaf. Their prison is the worldly ways of doing things, where greed and selfishness is seen as living a life of success.

Pride consumes the life of the lost, with arrogance that says," it is my way that is best." Most relationships fall apart because at the center is selfishness and greed. I have seen marriages where there is competition between the husband and the wife, when the focus should be on how to lift each other up. A house divided cannot stand. When marriages are bedeviled with such un-Godly antithesis there can never be any hope of survival. This is why we must be clear in asking God the question, "is this the one for me," and we must wait to hear from God. To marry anyone out of convenience or pity is a disservice to the other person and to yourself. It is a loosing game that causes too much pain and heartache which does not please God.

In our business relationship with others we must ask the question, "How Lord can my activity honor you? I do know that there are Christians who are in businesses where honesty is frowned at because they profit from deception. My advice to such persons is where the environment is tolerable, honor God by being the light that shines amongst the darkness. Where that is impossible because the malpractice is entrenched, then seek an alternative place of employment. I have been offered ways of circumvention but at the end of the day my question is does it honor God, or can I live with myself? Over the years I have modeled that peace and integrity come first in what it means to be a true servant of God, and this matters more than quick ascension. Whatever is not of God eventually crumbles. Businesses that gain by dishonest measures have a way of corrupting the surrounding community and ultimately causing a breakdown in society.

This chapter reminds me of some of the same ills that go on in my country of birth, Nigeria. This is a country I love dearly, for Nigeria is beautiful, and her people are fun to be around. Many of them love the Lord deeply, I may dare say. It is a place where worship of God and giving, is done with jubilation and zest. Also there are few among them who are just religious and dubious. A country endowed with abundance of earthly and human resources and wealth, yet the wicked corrupted heart of many is everywhere, and within the church which is paroxysmal. The insatiable desire for richness at any means is destroying the land. Nigeria in this present time reminds me of the corruption in the divided kingdoms of Judah and Israel in the times of Jeremiah, Amos, Isaiah, and Ezekiel to mention a few. God warned repeatedly with His prophets that greed, selfishness, covetousness, and idolatry would be the ruin of the people if they did not listen. God punished the land with the cloak of captivity. But my heart grieves for Nigeria as a mother and a father grieves for their loved ones. I remain prayerful for the nation and like other Nigerians in Diaspora, and the remnants in the country, who are crying out for justice and whose hearts are grieved for the reckless abandonment that walks the corridors of the society, as it appears no one cares, but God is watching. It is truly troubling when the desires of the many are well intentioned and a few breed the rottenness that seems to thrive. Nigeria is a country where I cannot wait to have a permanent fixture in ministry and with physical presence. Many of the masses have become worshipers of men and followers of superstitious religions instead of God. While respect is part of the culture, but when that respect is not based in righteousness, integrity, and honor, the society is in a wicked state.

Nigeria is a place where men and women of God are honored to a fault, that even when the crimson of their sin runs from their hair strands to the tips of their toe nails, they will not speak a word against God's chosen servant. Grant it, I truly believe that men and women of the cloth are not honored in the United States as they ought to, yet the level of blindness is a problem where there are abuses of the saints. My hope is that servants of God will rise to know the purpose behind the questions. I must state here, that we are always to worship God above all things alone and not our fellow mankind, but honor our leaders where honor is due.

It is not about dishonor, not about disloyalty, it is about clarification and understanding of the unknown so that the truth is spoken. Children of God should know the purpose behind the question is to honor God that we may be right with Him in all our aspirations.

The purpose behind the questions is to walk in light instead of darkness. Our life has a meaning when that life is in God and His purpose; a life without meaning is a life without God. God desires His children to live and walk according to His will, for His purpose, and to ask questions to make sure that we are in line with God. The purpose behind the question is that we may not lean to our own understanding but unto God. When we ask questions we are seeking to strengthen our faith and increase identity, or shore-up our assurance in God. But in our pursuit of this we should always make our request for support go together with an attitude of faith, obedience and humility.

The God that understands our weakness will most times respond to us through His love and grace. The ones who do not have reverence for God are those who do not ask questions. But those with Godly fear and the faithful children of God understand that it is proper to ask questions. In my personal journey and relationship with God, I have many times been confronted with moments of uncertainty in challenging situations. These times in my life when I experience uncertainty, the reassuring thing for me has been to know that God is there to encourage me and strengthen me.

Just two or few days ago a man named David met me around 3.00am in the morning. Out of his mouth the LORD spoke to encourage me as he delivered messages to me reaffirming what God has spoken to me. For me this day felt heavenly, as I was reassured and renewed in His Strength boosting my fearlessness to march on. We must ask questions if we are faithful Christians because it is in the palm of His Hands that heaven and earth will forever be known and can only be found.

Chapter 5

Mechanical Manufactured Church Events-Crusades

The mechanical manufactured church events-crusades are mostly void of the Spirit of God and lack direction. The purposes for such events are for those who organize them and their cohorts. Churches in Nigeria and throughout the world are burdened with crusades and some have carried the mannerism of weekly crusades to the United States. These transportations are no less feeble. These crusades are always in three-day secessions of Friday, Saturday, and Sunday. Around the world, in Nigeria in particular, they sometimes run through the week. I do not remember calling fellow soldiers of the Cross without hearing "I was on a crusade" or "we are having a crusade."

I have for awhile now been agitated pondering whether these crusades are of God or if some are nothing but orchestrate events. I am aware that when it is man-made nothing much, if anything, comes out of them. If crusade in its definitions means a cause, what is the cause? If it is a battle, which we know quite often we deal with spiritual battles at all times, how come transformation from the church is not happening? Instead corruption, wickedness, dubiousness are ever so pervasive. If it is a war or to bat down the flesh, why is it that adultery, fornication and the likes is ever so prevalent in the church? If it is fight, what then is the church not fighting against? If it is of movement, has the church moved away from their calling of being the conscience of the society responsible for the rich and the poor, the widows, widowers, and the prisoners (physical and spiritual)? If it is a struggle are we as the body of believers called the church in a deep struggle? Or maybe it is the campaign that the church has been holding just to win members without actually attaining conversion (which is what truly transforms the society and the people).

Have some of these crusades amounted to nothing than mere charades of crusade parades and why have the laypeople not been truly converted? We constantly hear of crusade events (another adjective used is "program"). The churches especially in Nigeria are wrapped-up with too many programs where the individual spiritual lives of the people no longer exist. It is difficult to find even one with a transparent life. Some of these people run in the corridors of the building called church, where they have lost their mind, and even lost the understanding that they are the church. I have known occasions where people are so involved in these church events doing church programs that they neglect their loved ones sick at the hospital. What makes them think that God is pleased with such behavior? It saddens me, but it proves their self-indulgence and ignorance of the Word. Without a relationship with the Lord, they set themselves up in place of God peddling their hollow religion that will never set people free. They are nothing more than hollow religious celebrities. Why these people are not asking questions and are not fed-up with this nonsense is something that I am not surprised of. For a great many in our time are victims and fall for the entertainment instead of substance, and being spoon-fed rather than seeking the truth on their own.

The society has not progressed in holiness, not in corruption free living, nor in truth telling. There are more wickedly acts done by those who are in the church and the performers, called people in leadership. In the same vain, pride, arrogance, and corruption have gripped the political leadership, so also some of the leaders in the churches. The society is not impacted by the "socialization: of churches with daily activities because most are just that mechanical manufactured church events-crusades, they are not led by God whose power is the only thing that impacts and changes lives. When churches spend most of their time as business men and women, in the secular society it is no surprise why there is no affect. We as a body of believers must realize that while God has always used human beings in His work on earth, the work of the church is about God and it is God and His people. To act like it is the work of humanity which is done with physical strength and philosophical understanding, is to be foolish. While we as humans bring some of these on board by doing the work of the ministry, at all times we must never fail in our reliance on God whose Spirit equips and leads us to do His work.

Over the years those that have known me and my relationship with the Lord, with their support of good intentions, have asked me to host events in the area of healing- revival or crusades of sort. I have always been reluctant because I have no interest in mechanically manufactured occasions or crusades that the Lord has not directed me to. These events should be done with God leading whom He has called out for such, and when this is not the case, the result is unmistakably just a show. Success will follow in any event or crusade that is of God. Revival will shake down the walls and turn the society around and on its head despite the resistance and rebellious forces of darkness that try to stand against the things of God. And so, I choose to be led and directed by God who has called me for this task. I am continually in prayer over my position with God and His choice of how He uses me for His glory. The practices of God are in His sovereign will.

More than hundred years ago, in 1906to be exact, in Los Angeles, William Seymour led the Azusa Street Revival and people are still talking and writing about it. The Welsh revival (1904–1905), was one of the largest gatherings of Christian revival during the 20th century; and other documented known revivals are recorded because those people allowed the leading of the Lord in their work. The events in these revivals or movements did not happen overnight, nor did anyone reading their stories find that it was their own mechanical making. These people spent countless years sacrificing, suffering, and in an unwavering devotion to God in prayer and the Lord showed up leading the way for His glory. There were healings with full manifestations of God's presence that destroys the hate, producing true transformation of lives.

Now that I have written on some of the ills I want to write to some of these church leaders and advise that to be *called* is to be led by God, who has chosen you for the assignment. If you are unsure of your role in the name of Jesus, please seek Godly counsel and find an appropriate mentor. Leaders lead with others along their side who are leading, and God directs; Leaders with the Spirit of God lead with a sacrificial heart of peace, patience, humility, forgiveness, kindness, giving, and above all, the Love of God.

To the body, the church, the saints, to honor and respect the leaders does not mean to be gullible. You as the children of God have all that it takes through the grace of God to know the truth; that truth is God. Your ability in knowing Him is to know His Word through reading the Bible. Faith comes by hearing the Word of God, but truth comes by knowing Him and that knowing is what makes you free from every lie that deceitful men and women will present to you, so that when their theatrics are nothing but mechanical theatrics, you will know. And so, my counsel is that in these times that the wisdom of God will be the guide to us all in all things as we go forth.

Our present day mechanical manufactured events-crusades or programs should have the direction of God with Jesus as the focus, where the unrighteous will come trembling with fear to the Lord for His redemption seeking new purpose for a new life. A year or two has gone by since I was again invited to a program after many invitations. Some of the speakers there needed spiritual deliverance, and sitting in the audience I was shaking my head because of what the Lord was revealing. One of those speaker's activities with women in the church would later be told to me and my reply was, "I am not surprised." There is something wrong to be invited to a crusade-event or program where some of the speakers are serial adulterers and fornicators in the church, where the leading organizers are of questionable character and where the love of Christ is nowhere to be found. A genuine crusade-event or program comes from serious men and women who are Spirit- filled, led of God, and directed by the Lord. It is not designed for mere fundraising purposes as some that I have witnessed, and I have often made it clear if the aim is to raise money, be up-front and clear with God's children. I desire not to partake in any and all events or programs other than where God is leading the path. The greatest days of the Church have been the days of revival. Nothing can take its place. The good and the best that man can do will never be enough. God is the only one who arrives on the scene in revival power, and then the church becomes a witness to a providence that has been promised.

Chapter 6

The Converted Life

A converted person is a transformed person. A believer who is transformed is a believer converted. This means for one to turn around from their old ways of lifestyle, to a new one. It means to transport oneself from one belief to another. Many including myself, have written on the conversion of Saul (Jewish name), to Apostle Paul (his Christian name). His conversion was of an amazing narrative and a true work of transformation of the faithful and for the glory of God. But, in this chapter and for this book, I want to focus on the life of a man in the gospel of Luke 19:1. The transformed Zaccheus is another story of conversion for the Christian faith. He was a chief tax collector who was hated in his community because of his line of work. For all intents and purposes he was a very wealthy man who was responsible for a commercial trading center. He may have had others who worked under him in this district of Jericho and how large the district was, we may not know in our time.

The focal point here is the conversion of this wealthy man, Zaccheus. The Bible tells us that he was a small stature of a man who possibly could have been concealed in the crowd and not have been seen by Jesus. Not risking his chance of meeting Jesus, and not knowing whether such opportunity would ever present itself again, in his determination and desire to be converted he climbed on the low limb of a sycamore tree. It was there that Jesus took notice of him high on the tree and said, "Zaccheus, hurry and come down, for today I must stay at your house (Luke 19:5)." Zaccheus was a man who did not allow anything to stand in his way and he was well known in his community and wealthy. But now he shed the shroud of human status seeking in exchange his conversion. At this point of humility, the Bible tells us that Jesus took notice probably not only of Zaccheus' outward physical demonstration of determination, but very likely Jesus saw his heart. Zaccheus committed himself in repentance to Jesus as we read in Luke 19:8, "Behold, Lord, half of my possessions I will give to the poor, and if I have defrauded anyone of anything, I will give back four times as much." The willingness here was without compulsion demonstrating a genuine heart of conversion. The Bible tells the story that the act here by Zaccheus was more than required. For the law held his penalty at one-fifth for the crime of money illegally obtained by fraud. Zaccheus takes his further beyond the law of jurisdiction making a costly commitment with a true evidence of a changed man.

May I also point out here that Zaccheus may have been aware of the Word of the Lord spoken by prophet Ezekiel, "If the wicked restores the pledge, gives back what he has taken by robbery, walks in the statues of life, committing no iniquity; he shall live, he shall not die (Ezekiel 33:15)." Jesus knew this part of His law but this is where those who were against Jesus for embracing Zaccheus missed it. All they beheld to was that Zaccheus was a sinner; but they did not see beyond that. Jesus had to remind them through His action, that salvation was for the lost- those who repent and turn away from their sinful ways.

Saints of God, *it is what you are willing to give up that reveals your true conversion.* Sacrificial commitment cannot occur until the heart is repentant, and once that change of heart occurs then the work of transformation begins to manifest within and around you, whether in secret or in the open. The true repentance of the believer brings with it spiritual blessings to the family, individually and corporately.

This begs the question whether all Christians are truly converted people of God. The answer is no. There are so many who are Christians by association; they love the identification. They may on occasion visit the church, but they are not in any way repentant in their hearts. There are also those who are Christians because it has become for them a family tradition. Mom and Dad took them to church from little age, and for them they have a tradition to sustain giving the impression that the family is a Christian family because they go to church on Sundays. Sadly to say that various ways are plausible expressed avenues of Christian identification; and yet these families and individuals are not anywhere, in any way, close to being converted persons to tell the truth.

In the true meaning of converted person or persons transformed, if most who call themselves Christians were truly transformed, the world we live in would indeed be a different world. Rather what we have within our churches are some, if not many, who are lukewarm Christians. They walk in disobedience with no real commitment in the exercise of their faith. Others are there for the social gathering thrilled by the entertainment value and the contacts they have established. A small remnant is the true converted or transformed people who take their faith and their walk seriously. These are those who are like Zaccheus, with deep repentant hearts in true reverential fear for the Lord and devotion. They have a sense of commitment and obligation to mend their wrongs, and are ready for the redemption of a new walk with our Lord and Savior Jesus Christ. These are those people who make others around them feel the vibrant essence of God's love all around; they show it by loving others. If half of those who claim they are Christian are found with a converted heart there would be less hate especially among Christians instead of the hate one finds among so-called Christians. There would not be any church in some parts of the world where racism would be found. I would like to say that any place that calls itself a church and practices racism and segregation is NOT A CHURCH OF GOD. What God hates is sin but God does not hate his creation and for any to hate their fellow mankind and claim the right to know God, it is a fraud. No hate can be found in God.

Briefly to write on Apostle Paul, his conversion is one of the most spoken of in the Bible. Here was a man who persecuted Christians and the fact is he was on his way to discomfort more when he met

Jesus. His conversion from Judaism to the knowledge of the true God changed his being and his worldview of what it meant to have the love of God. God not only touched him in a mighty way, Apostle Paul learned to demonstrate God's love to those who were not part of the promise. There is no question that part of his being chosen was his zeal in Judaism. We must remember that Apostle Paul was an ardent believer in his Jewish faith, and his devotion may be responsible for God choosing him knowing that when touched the devotion drive that he had shown with Judaism that same zeal he would bring in conversion to the Christian faith.

Talking to an acquaintance recently, he said this to me, "The whole thing about apostles I believe was only for the first century church," But he does not have an explanation for the gifts of the Spirit (which names apostles) mentioned over and over in the New Testament. I do not want anyone to think it is about the title of an apostle that I am hung up on. I just do not understand how we can choose part of the Bible and deny the other in the same breath. This is the Word of God; the very foundation that our faith is based upon. It is in the same Bible that the office of a pastor is given and we for some strange reason are comfortable with pastor and not apostle. A wise man or woman will stop right now and open 1Corinthians 12:28, and Ephesians 4:11, and read with their own eyes. It appears to me that people seek to remain with what is familiar to them. For one to experience the supernatural things of God, we must be willing to deny our prideful attachment to humanism; this idea that man knows it all.

Now, turning back to Zaccheus, there was not much written about Zaccheus, but in the text he went on with his life blessing the poor with half of his riches. Zaccheus gained in spiritual riches and was willing to part with half of his earthly material possession. There is a lesson here for believers. That lesson is to know that going to church without a mind made-up to receive and be transformed, yet claiming to know Jesus is hollow, and there can be no conversion. But a mind that is made-up and ready, Jesus will always find. And when one is found He will begin to dine with that one. I said this in my previous book and I write here to express my own personal experience that my life has not been the same after God touched me. The question of God's power cannot be fully written in describable terms of His impact in my life, but there is also a willing part of me to yield to the ways of God to do the work for which He began in me before I was formed in my mother's womb. Like in the life of Apostle Paul and Zaccheus these are characters discussed here that were willing to yield to God to be used.

Ironically, in Luke chapter 18, Jesus had just dealt with a young rich ruler who was in love with his earthly possessions and couldn't let go. But when reading about Zaccheus we find a rich man who was not only willing to let his riches go to cover his sins, but he also gave to the poor. Jesus used the young rich ruler to explain how hard it is for a rich man to enter into the kingdom of heaven. And in our present day we see it. Most rich people worship their wealth, and are dismissive of anything about God and the less fortunate amongst them are seen as less than a human being. This goes to prove what Jesus expressed to the young rich ruler. But Zaccheus was quite willing to let go of some of his earthly possessions; how willing are you? I have laid out my sacrifice and my continued journey in the hope that I may fully attain His glory. I leave you with this, know that a converted heart yields, and a converted heart and life says, no matter the cost I will follow You. A converted heart and life says, not my will but Your will Oh' Lord!.

Chapter 7

What is it That You are Exercised About? (Motive)

What we are exercised about makes a difference in each of our lives. It is an indicator of who we are and what is important to us....it is the motive that sometimes may be unspoken. What is it that you are exercised about is the, "I beg your pardon" that brings out the question that is asked. I am known to ask questions and come alive because I am exercised by what is most important in my life, and that is my passion for Jesus.

Recently, visiting my cousin-in-law who has been battling cancer and sadly lost his battle before my finishing *I Hear You!...But What is God Saying?*; my wife and her cousin and his wife entered into a conversation for probably about ten minutes or so without my participation. My wife turns to me in her loving manner with a smile and says, "Where are you in this and where have you traveled to?" I replied, nowhere; I stated that I was only trying to respect their conversation since they were getting reacquainted on family history. With this, all eyes turned to me for participation. As we laughed at this moment me not even knowing now what was said, a conversation about God was raised and immediately I found myself rushing into it, and my wife said, "Now we got his attention since it is about God." And she was right. I have always asked what else I should be excited about other than my area of endeavor. But I tell this story because this is what I am exercised about in my life. Most marriage relationships fall apart when one of the partners is exercised not by the success of the marriage in terms of the sacrifices and sharing, but by money. So many marriages in ministry fall apart, not because the wife or husband is not called, but because one of them is exercised much about money-making and well-doing, therefore spiritual growth for the ministry takes the back seat.

To find myself exercised in anything other than God and His ways will mean that I am in a wrong place and in a wrong calling. So I am exercised by the things of God and to have me talking is to talk about God. Most of you who are preachers or have been in the church circle long enough will be familiar with this saying, 'Ask a preacher a question, or ask them to speak.' you will never hear the end. Reason being that they love to talk or are always preaching, this is simplistic inference. The overall hidden reason here may be that many of these preachers are people of deep passion and conviction. I will say it is a place that I plead guilty as charged; when it comes to the things about God my fervor is immeasurable and uncontainable.

Finding myself engrossed with any topic other than what I do or have been anointed to do, will prove where my heart is. Not yet in too many instances have I seen or found one who is not consumed by the areas of their expertise or endeavor. Medical doctors find pride in medicine. Lawyers can not help but let you know they are lawyers. Engineers always show their ability in methodological behavior, and Psychologists want us to believe that they have all the answers. The reason here being that these people are proud of their professions and so they're exercised. The clergy or preacher whose assignment is genuine and is called of God will demonstrate their passion and if it is possible, in all they do it will be about God.

However, there is a problem when someone claims they are God's servant but they are not exercised by the Word of God or things relating to the church, but by business or money. Hearing of an incessant statement from a preacher about the stock market and investment reveals that the heart is in a place other the work of God. I write to say do not misunderstand me; I do know the need for money and its relevance. No church can function without money including the one that the Lord has allowed me to shepherd for His glory. But the truth must be that God makes available the resources to do His work. It may not come in a trailer-truck and at the time we want it, however it will come if we are trusting in Him. To be exercised in business or making money becomes the red flag that this person is there not to serve the Lord, but to be served with what they can get. The Bible warns of what awaits every foundation not established by God. Jesus Christ in His teaching states simply in Matthew 15:13-14, "Every plant which My heavenly Father did not plant shall be uprooted. Let them alone; they are blind guides of the blind. And if a blind man guides a blind man, both will fall into a pit." Meaning here is that the end for such ministry and their leaders is destined to fall apart. In the initial stages such ministries may appear successful and glamorous but God uproots that fame and status in no far-flung time.

Every act, the nakedness of all is before God and His wrath is upon all ungodliness of the wicked men and women who choose to suppress the truth. To be exercised by something other the service of God and His people for those in church leadership, is deceitful and evil. God requires accountability of those who are in the ministry for the lives of His people who have been deceived and duped at their hands for they are clearly not exercised by the work of God but by their own motive and agenda. They are the bad shepherds and this is spoken in Ezekiel 34:10, "Thus says the Lord God: "Behold, I am against the shepherds, and I will require My flock at their hand; I will cause them to cease feeding the sheep, and the shepherds shall feed themselves no more; for I will deliver My flock from their mouths, that they may no longer be food for them." What God is saying here is that He is in control of all situations, even when it looks as if prosperity is in the hands of these deceitful men and women, God's plan will cause them to cease. In the midst of what looks successful, is the judgment of God upon them. There are those whose interpretation of this text is that it was only for the people at that period seeing what God did in the life of King Zedekiah in our reading of Jeremiah 52:10-11, but we know that the Word of God is a warning for all times including this present time.

I want to bring to conclusion this chapter with simple advice to those who are aspiring to be in the ministry. But before my advice I want to state clearly that if you have been called from the body of your own mother's womb, God will give you the strength no weather the storm, to endure it all. And I know always that when He chooses one for His work ones heart will be inclined to please Him. For those who are not sure of their calling but love the work of the ministry, while your desire may be good, know that the desire alone may not sustain you in doing this work we call 'the work of ministry.' Be aware that ministry and the work of ministry are not for those whose goal in life is to become materially successful. If that is the reason why you desire to be in ministry, you might as well seek something other than this. Be exercised for what you have been called to do and aspire to do it well like none other can. Seek what you will become the best at in the area of your endeavor, and if ministry is not your work, seek something other through the counseling of those you trust. Stop the worrying of somebody else's ministry, or trying to emulate what they are doing and how. Rejoice in seeing your brother and sister in faith rise to the occasion and be used for the glory of the one who has called them. Too many have spent time and money secretly coveting. And some even overtly try to become copy-cats of other churches, their style, and their preaching style, so that their success may become like those others. God is not pleased. Covetousness is not of God but demonic. You will be used and can be used, if called for that which the LORD has written in your book of destiny.

Chapter 8

God, Why Not Use Me as You Use Him/Her?

God says, no I will not 'use you as I use him or her,' because how I use him or her is my business and I have called them in those assignments for my own glory. I will use you how I choose to use you because how I use you I, God, have decided that this is what I have called you for and the only way I have chosen to use you for my honor. To seek otherwise is to be disobedient towards God and of the calling. It is a sin to seek what is not yours. It is covetousness in the same category as thieves; it is representing a moral failure and a characteristic of an unsaved person. So many in the body who are Christians or claim to be, are found with these flaws and disappointedly many of these people are in leadership. Some of these leaders even surmise, "Since God doesn't speak to me I must not be very important to Him" (this is nothing but a rebellious spirit). God speaks to each person in His own time in different ways which may be through His written Word, through other ministry leaders, etc. But this thought is not the issue. Some leaders and people in general, must understand that the human concept of time means nothing to God. When it is too late for mankind it may not be too early for God. The Lord searches the pure heart of a man and woman before He assigns them. What's more, those hearts even as imperfect as they may be, must be bendable to God to be used for His glory.

Let me be lucid to state that a desire with a heart of truth, kindness and love is a longing that God honors, and is pleasing to Him. But those who envy and are jealous of others for who they are in the Lord are a vexation of the Spirit. Apostle Paul gives us the description vividly in 1 Corinthians 3:3, "For you are still of the flesh. For while there is jealousy and strife among you, are you not of the flesh, and behaving like ordinary men?" This portrayal is of a great many in the church and the church leadership. God does not honor such a craving, and these people at some point or another become disillusioned and walk away from ministry. I have seen so many of these people. They do not like others in faith because they are jealous of their positions and are unsure of themselves.

They are people who float with attitude like this, well' if I cannot be used like them I do not want them around me. They are people constantly worried of their position and fearfully fearing at every present moment that other ministers will out-shine them. Some of these people dare not call you by the office that God has given you, but rather they strategize you into a familiar social status that is comfortable and convenient to them.

These leaders with evil, possessive grips cannot stand to see other ministers talking to their members because they are worried they will loose them to another ministry. I recall telling some of these people to first have the sense of self-assurance in who they are in God; if they do not know of themselves then they are to seek clearance from God of who they are in Him. In my last book writing somewhat on this problem with the clergy, I used a phrase that "I pray if any is enslaved that they need to seek to know who they are in the Lord" and that truly is my wish. I have yet to understand why anyone called of God should be angry when people leave their church. Our job as servants of God, called of God, is to always pray that as they leave that they by the grace of God will be implanted in another ministry where they are washed by the Word of God and for God's glory.

To be disappointed is natural and this I understand because I have seen over the years people who tell me, "oh' Apostle I am with you to the end of time." It was almost like they were saying, "I will be with you until when Jesus comes," and only to see them walk away from the church. I cannot begin to count the number of people whom I thought were inseparable with me only to see them walk away with no care. Am I disappointed? Oh' yes, especially when time and energy has been invested in their spiritual growth. Seeing them walk away becomes painful but this should not be for a moment a place that festers anger or hate. Church leaders, hear this, those who leave your church for another, belong to God. They are the children of God who have a right to attend any church and fellowship anywhere of their own choosing. Question might be asked, what happened to commitment and loyalty? Great questions but can anyone force loyalty? Can you force one whose vision is not twined with yours? The answer that will be simple is this, can two walk together, talk when they do not agree with a common purpose? I do not at any moment seek to have around me people who are not loyal to the cause that I pursue or the vision that the LORD has given to me. So it makes sense for us to allow God to draw to us those whom He has called out to serve with us.

Hand-picked men and women, chosen by God do not need much convincing to see the vision and to then align with it. These kinds serve with conviction. Their loyalty is unquestionable, and they are trustworthy. They come on board to do the will of God in service and truth; their desire is not one of covetousness. When others stir the choppy waters of weakness what is found in Godly Christians is a conviction that is resolute. They are in essence Christians who know that a true leader comes through service. God always lifts these quality people or persons up to take the reign of the mantle of leadership in due season. There is a parable that states, "One who walks with a king is one who becomes a king." First that King is Jesus as we walk with Him in obedience, and with a heart of love He lifts us up. God not only lifts up His own in promotion but also those who follow in service to His chosen ones, they are lifted –up in their season.

This example is given to us through the lives of some in the Bible and one of whom is a man called Joshua. Joshua's life is that of a true servant, loyal to the chosen one called by God named Moses. Throughout the Bible there are hardly any verses where we read of disagreement between Joshua and Moses. The Bible tells us in

Deuteronomy 34:9, "Now Joshua the son of Nun was filled with the spirit of wisdom, for Moses had laid his hands on him; and the sons of Israel listened to him and did as the LORD had commanded Moses." Joshua was a servant who knew what it meant to support the one chosen; succession of leadership at the end of the services of Moses death eventually was bestowed upon him. God chose Joshua to lead the children of Israel to the promise land. Leaders are chosen by God; they do not covet. They are people who serve without self-ambition, and they serve the one called to serve, and the people. They do not occupy themselves with the question of, "God, why not use me as you use that person or this person; nor ask why I can't be like that one." They are content in service, knowing their place and who they are.

There is another biblical example of transfer in leadership for the church. It is that of Elisha, from Prophet Elijah in 2 Kings 2, Prophet Elisha stood with Prophet Elijah for the order of succession had to come through God. 2 Kings 2:5b reveals God at work with those whom He chooses. God had made known to Prophet Elisha that he was to call home Prophet Elijah. The scripture states that when the sons of the prophet told Elisha that God was about to permanently take away Elijah, Elisha replied, "Yes, I know; be still." Throughout Prophet Elijah's interactions with him, Prophet Elisha swore to him to stand behind or besides his master Prophet Elijah. The submission of the Prophet Elisha to Prophet Elijah to the end is the same submission that came from the sons of the prophets to Prophet Elisha when in (v15), the spirit of Elijah rested on that of Elisha. But the beauty of this transfer of power for me climaxed in 2 kings 2:9, "when they had crossed over, Elijah said to Elisha, ask what I shall do for you before I am taken from you." And Elisha said, "Please, let a double portion of your spirit be upon me." The Bible states that Elijah's reply was that Elisha had asked for a hard thing. But he said, "Nevertheless, if you see me when I am taken from you, it shall be so for you; but if not, it shall not be so."

There is here this revelation in the order of transfer from Elijah who acknowledges that what he had was not his to give; but God who has given was to be the One to transfer the power accordingly in accordance with His will. This is where in our time the church and the so called leaders' aspirers who are covetous in every way are missing completely. They in their own covetous spirit will in some instances sabotage their own blessings by destroying a ministry or the one whom they thought is in their way, invariably denying themselves what could have been theirs. It reminds me of a parable in my Ikwerre ethnic language from Nigeria. It goes this way, "A monkey that resides on trees and leaps from tree to tree sees the trees uprooted and falling. The monkey is rejoicing with laughter but never did the monkey know his house was falling because soon there would not be a place for the monkey to call home." Elisha was not anxious about the eminent departure of his master nor was he overly happy, but he remained patient and served and the blessing in due course was passed on to him. So also must our present leadership aspirers be patient else they miss their blessing.

Some time ago, a similar event of "God why not use me as him/her," occurred in our church. One who was an assistant thought that my position was theirs to have. I sensed the embellishment and greedy behavior but naively I was of the thinking that with time this too shall pass. But God was not accepting it, and the LORD spoke and said, "When ever you stand to speak that one thinks it is about you, but they have failed to see that it is not you who speaks, but Me who is at work through you." God said, "do not say a word and do not lift your finger, I am about to remove them from you, and when I do, don't go asking them to come back." As the LORD spoke so it happened and it was not long in the manifestation of this person's removal from our church. The problem with this mind-set of 'God why them and why not me' or 'why not use me as you them' is that it is covetous, evil, and it is greediness. These people are demonically led. These people are in all circles in our society and especially in Church leadership. They are people not satisfied with what is given to them and what they have is never good enough. Lord 'why not use me as you use him or her' are dangerous people. Whether they are in your family, in your community, in the secular work place, or the church leadership, they are miserable, restless, and unhappy, and they lack Joy. They are always the tools of the wicked one. And these branches of people are by nature very egotistic; to them it is not about the true love of God it is about their self-image.

God help us.

Chapter 9

Be in the World, But Not of it. Why?

Whereas the central theme in the Bible is about sin of the world, and the redeemed in Christ called the believers, we are commanded to be out of the world. It is in that context we are admonished not to adhere to the ways of the world. We are to be in it as the salt of the earth; as the light that shines in midst of darkness. For this title and in this chapter I will try as much as possible to discuss what this means for the church, the life of the redeemed, and our role to be in the world, and why not of it. As the salt of the earth, we are to be a seasoning or a preserver. Salt is used in food to bring out flavor, a taste to the food, that taste is adding something good, not bad. A salt as a preserver protects the food from harm, not cause damage to it. As Christians we are called to preserve. We are supposed to save not spoil; to turn what had the predisposition of spoiling to maintaining it for the immediate or for future good use. Our being in the world is of this mandate and that is the whole point of why we are called the salt of the earth. When Christians are failures in functionality as the salt, we are of the world, and to be of the world is to be of no good use as a person of faith.

Time and again I have run into men and women in ministry who are of the world. They are in most cases a disgrace to the faithful people of God, and the entire body as a community known as the church. To be so money hungry leaves nothing desirable in the life of one who claims they have been called. Men or women of the cloth, who do not love but are cranky and selfish, should not seek the work of the ministry. This work is such that calls for sacrifice and selfless living. To be in the ministry and not love people begs the question how one could have even found oneself in the ministry to begin with in the first order of thinking.

The whole idea of why the Word of God has commanded us to be in the world is nothing more, nothing less, but for us to demonstrate the life of our Lord and Savior Jesus Christ to those who are lost in the world; and that life can only be shown through His Love demonstrated by those that love Him. This action of love must be not in exclusion of truth, obedience, holy living, patience, endurance, integrity, righteousness and justice to those we meet out there. Through us in the world salvation is demonstrated through our works to those outside who might not have come to know Jesus Christ. I have also realized that unfortunately some of the most trusted allies that one will find may not be in the church but outside of it. Personally, some of the people who have proven as true friends have not been those in the church or my fellow clergy, rather they are men and women of amiable character who are in various other professions. Here I want to make clear what a true friend is about.

A true friend is a friend who will not be afraid to answer the door bell in the middle of the night. This friend is the friend who without hesitation gives the shirt off their back for the other; a person of character and integrity this cuts both ways for the true friendship to be. To walk with one who calls themselves your friend but constantly one is watching their back, is to be with an enemy who was never a friend to begin with. Too often in the ministry I have come to experience people who call you their friends but their heart is farther from what it means to be a friend. This kind of friend and relationship is empty and has no foundation in God. Maybe we in this period in time where relationships are too transactional no longer know what the word friend means; the Webster defines *friend*, "a person whom one knows well and is fond of, an ally, supporter, or sympathizer." Maybe it is the transactional state of being that has led to a diminished meaning of a 'friend.' I have had for years now a joke commonly told between my wife and me. This became a joke later, but it was a shock to me when it happened. A man of faith, whom I have admired, respected and considered a friend, was moving from his place of residence unbeknown to my wife and me. We were walking the street we live on when we saw they were moving. We asked where they were moving to. The answer we received was, "ten blocks away from here." At that moment I did not know what to make of this evasive answer. My conclusion was simply, there was no relationship to begin with and there it ended until this writing. I have never seen or heard from them and so my wife and I often pass by the street and jokingly say …. "Ten blocks away from here." Now, I have come to the understanding that many of these people are mere companions (nothing more than one who accompanies you) who share the same common interest. An example of the true biblical definition of what a friend is can also be found in the relationship of David and Jonathan in 1 Samuel 20. True friendship is not evasive, does not lie to another, seeks the well being of the other with honesty and sincerity, and will seek what is in the best interest of the other; it is not based on competition and should never be based on what we have in material possessions. It should be based on love with mutual respect and that love should be of Christ Jesus.

The love of God is selfless, meaning that it is not about self-fulfillment but it is for the well-being of the children of God. It is in this context that greed and selfishness becomes the reproach to the life of one who thinks about nothing but their own well-being. I am not seeking to deny the importance of the well-being of the priest or the chosen men and women of God, not in the least. I also must mention and employ saints of God that the well-being of the husbands and wives of those who have been chosen to serve are just as equally important as their own. To always seek their help and counsel and not be a blessing to their lives may be equally a sinful act.

The priest, the chosen servants of God, must at all times be provided for; for a worker is entitled to pay. And in this case the Word of God makes it crystal clear all through the Bible, beginning with God in Genesis setting aside the Levites the priestly family to be provided for by the entire tribes. And in our time, the churches are the tribes through the New Testament with scriptures laying out the commandments we ought to follow when priests, all those who labor in ministry, teach and pastor us in the Spiritual things. They are worthy of financial and material blessings. It is not about paying somebody else in our modern day in the ministry, it is about the one whom God has used to bless our lives, and the one He has called to lead us. Just as we know to pay doctors, lawyers, psychologist, and Psychiatrists, etc., etc., men and women of God called to serve must be paid.

Focusing back on 'be not of the world' for a moment, we priest or leaders of the church must display the love of God in every aspect of our lives. Our word must be our worth. A man or woman of God whose word means nothing cannot be trusted. A higher moral character is to be expected of us in words and in deeds, and must be found in our lives. To be a liar is to live a lie of your calling and God who has called you. Quite frequently some men and women of God who claim they are called, speak and their words are as hollow as an empty barrel because they have proven over and over that they cannot live up to their words. They lack the truth, they cannot be trusted. When our assistance is sought after in cases of family discrepancy, we should strive to be honest brokers of peace as God would want us at all times, whether it is in marital discord or any other area and where you are confronted with temptation, learn to flee by reassigning the position of counseling to others. Do not covet; for such destroys your position for which you have been called. By bringing disgrace and shame to God, you destroy your family and bring disrepute to the office to which you have been called.

To be in the world if we are true to our faith, draws us to people who love God, but for some reason they are at a point where they cannot get their act together by finding their way back to Jesus and walking in it. Sometimes they are people who for some time have desired to know Jesus and have been waiting to meet the one who may be used to explain to them the Word of God where finally they will be drawn in. To be in the world and not of it helps in many ways to bring healing to those who in times past may have been in the church but they have been bruised, wounded, and have left the family fold of faith, and now are looking for reassurance that what they may have previously experienced was not of God, and not a true representation of His will for their lives. We as people, the human race, are not created as an island. We as created beings are to enjoy others in our lives. We always have this great opportunity to learn from one another, if we will be willing to open ourselves up to one another. We have to expand our horizon in the learning of other things in this earthly realm which we call our world. While we are created to glorify God at all times and places, when we are in the world and not of it, our first word may not be about God and the Bible, but just to learn how to carry a conversation on the issues of life, and share common interests may be all at a given moment there is or may be. As the salt of the earth, our lives are observed and watched while in the world. If we are indeed the salt of the earth there are great opportunities for us to be used to win-over those who are of the world around us. This is why we are commanded to be in the world, but not of it.

I pray that God will help us to be the earthly flavor; the salt of the earth.

Chapter 10

Ask, But Never Say Never

The longer many of us take stock of our life, if we are sincere, the more there will be that acknowledgement of learning not only to ask questions, but learning to never say the word *never* again. It becomes no longer a word to be uttered in our lives with the situations we face. In my life journey, personally and corporately, it is riddled with the shell of everything I said would never be part of me. It is in these moments of life experiences that I have learned not to say the word *never,* ever again. Brothers and sisters of the faith and in Christ Jesus, nobody amongst us knows what our future holds, and what that unknown future will bring to us at anytime. It is at this place in my half adult life existence on earth which appears quickly on the run from me, that I have seen that the plan of mankind is worthless except for the benevolent grace of God. Truly humankind may plan all they want but God executes, and this the Bible states clearly in Proverbs 19:9, "The mind of man plans his way, But the LORD directs his steps." I think we are reminded here that in all plans of the human race the sovereign God is the one who overrules the plans to fulfill His purposes.

If you recall in chapter four of *I Hear You!...But What is God Saying?*, I laid out the necessities of asking questions, but we must be aware that because we asked, whether to God or of our fellow human beings the questions, and the answers are given, it should not be interpreted that those answers are bonds that cannot be broken. These bonds of answers we receive will be broken by none other than

God, or your fellow human beings. You probably ask what I mean by God. Well, hear this, when God tells you to go that I am with you, God certainly is with you because God does not lie and He is indeed with you to the end. However along the road on the journey with God there are many moments and times where you wonder and will ask, "God! Where are you? Did you not say You are with me?" It is of these places and moments you as the individual will be confronted with the things that in many occasions you may have said you will not deal with. If you are one who has never been used to asking, be ready to ask. If you never thought to beg, pack your bags and know that you will beg. If you never dealt with a feeling of lack, realize the times of the sensations of lack will surround you. If you have a problem surrendering you will learn to surrender. And if pride has been one of your struggles in life, turn to your right quickly and embrace humility and humbleness immediately. I have learned to say to people now when I do hear them say the word, 'I will never do this and that' my answer to them is......don't you say it, because you never know. God in His wisdom will in every way allow us to be affronted with issues to teach us that life is nothing, but life is a mere shadow and that we are never confident of and never self-assured of in any stretch of imagination.

My realization in the dishonor meted to me by fellow servants of God, or people in general is that God uses these disappointments to refocus my attention on Him. Why? Even they in acting-out are unaware of the reasons why they dish out dishonor. And so, what I now do when confronted with such is to pray for their soul.

In our personal lives these are the humiliating lessons of life that most of us are never quite prepared for, nor even know what to make of it when this issues that are out of our control show-up at our front door step. I will not write here to explain completely how many times I have heard people confess in their vow never to be divorced, and find themselves in the divorce-dockyard. Some of these are folks who are believers with good intentions who have a great respect and the honor for the institution of marriage. Many of whom came from homes with a history of marriage as a lasting institution legacy. Yet in their own lives what they said never will happen because they have not learned to put God first and then others. Some in this marriages thought that God was in it, or at least they had confirmation from the Lord before the marriage, or maybe not. I will use myself as the example here.

My parents were married for well over sixty years before my father's journey home to glory. Growing up I was proud of the relationship that my parents exemplified for me and of the community I had grown up in, and rightfully so. I had sworn that I was to duplicate the same happy and peaceful marriage, but was I ever naïve, for divorce soon came for me calling. Even after many years of my waiting to make sure that marriage was going to be right, I found my self divorced. Looking back now, I have to know that all those times of my waiting were done in my own flesh, it was not the manner and how God wanted it for me.

I know a young man who confessed to me that until his marriage which happened in his late twenties, he was a virgin and his wife was the first woman known to him sexually. After more than ten years of marriage, they are now divorced. Without knowing what was involved and all that led to this chapter in his life, his pain was evident. He never thought divorce to be an option and now he is among the casualties of life pain called divorce.

These issues of life that we receive answers of promise with assurance will be broken after all the questions we ask and the disappointment will come from our family and most times from our children. Family members, brothers, and sisters will rise up against you to a degree that an outsider, an on-looker will asks the question, are you sure they are related? Most, not all families, experience jealousy and greed within the family before outside encumbrances occur. However, in my own family I have experienced a greedy family uncle with his ego who has determined not to see me succeed in the work that the LORD called me for. I laugh at him because the stool I sit on has been given to me by God not man and usually not him for nothing he has given and definitely nothing will he be able to take from me. My joy conversely to his madness is that God is equally determined to bring dishonor and shame to him with my success, because as God has sworn and said, "Surely, just as I have intended so it has happened, and just as I have planned so it will stand"(Isaiah 14:24). And with the children, they will do things that will cause the parents to ask, where is this coming from? It may not mean you are a bad parent; it does not mean that you never showered them with love. The reason may just be that in this life there is the tree of depravity, where all disobedience and rebelliousness started. In one form or the other we will have these challenges that will cause us to re-evaluate the meaning of life. Except to know God's grace and mercy which has helped us and our families, it is that love that is great towards us.

My wife and I were watching a Christian comedian with his jokes recently who said something that stuck with me. He said, "God gave us children (particularly in their teenage years) to see what it feels like to create something in your own image and see them not follow you." My experiences with my children may not have reached this place of conclusion or for me to know what the rest of their path in life will be, but my familiarity with them is quite a stack away from the way I related to my own parents. I know that most parents of this age will relate to my thinking here. I am also sure that if my one surviving parent were to be asked, they would confirm the delineation in my behaviors to theirs in the time of their own up-bringing. But surely I am aware that their testimony will be that experiences of the present are fairly chaotic.

It is in these relationships that we deal with that we experience things that make us learn to say, *never say never.* For at the turn of every point in our lives the relegation of life reminds us that we are not in control, therefore; we cannot be sure of what will be. It also helps us to be careful not to speak too soon in the life of others because we just never know what tomorrow might bring in our lives, with our children, and the people around us. The older I get the more I learn that in this life sometimes the apple you set your eyes on may turn to become a lemon and the oranges that looked so good and delicious maybe turn to become such a so, so, of a sour grape. It is only the grace of God that brings us through it all.

Growing up in my earthly Ikwerre culture and tradition I was taught that children belong to their parents only when they are still in the womb. Once they are out of the womb they belong to the world in service and to God in glory. Notice that I did not state, "they belonged to God before the world," but the truth is that they have always been God's. In this context what they will become is in the hand of God who already has known, even before the parents will begin to travel that road of wondering what they will become. I have deduced from my understanding and working relationship with God that as parents, our children are not ours as we claim but we are caretakers of them for God from whose hands these children and their life were given to begin with. Why we find it hard to accept the idea that our children belong to God and the world, is beyond me. Most times they do not follow our path in life anyway. As parents, our falsehood as people is refusing to acknowledge this very point of view.

The role for us is that of caretakers for God. We are to nurture and to be good stewards. Good stewards watch over and care for what has been entrusted into their hands for good care. We must never miss this about the children's lives we call *ours*; that they totally belong to the almighty God before we can call them ours. This is why God has admonished us to raise them up in His wisdom not with our worldly ways. Unfortunately, our depraved nature and our confused state of condition cause us to transmit the worldly wisdom instead of Godly wisdom. But we must come to the full understanding in raising them that the Word of God should be our first tool, whether in their lives or in our own lives. Those expectations of ours which we place on them should be checked outside the perimeter of our life form. All things must be subjected to the grace of God; because how they will turn-out we may never know and what will become of their lives and ours, we have no clue.

This is also the reason why as children ourselves to our parents, and our children to us, when death will come for us or our children, we do not know. Working on this chapter for *I Hear You!...But*

What is God Saying? the nation had experienced a tragedy that was devastating in 2013. It is the kind that has been frequent everywhere in the world but this time it was in Oklahoma. It is so painful, the hurt is unbearable. I am actually in tears when watching all kinds of natural disasters or the situations of frequent wickedness which humanity perpetrate on their own fellow human beings. However, talking to one friend I told him that situations like these cause us to reassess what is important in our lives. Most of those had their homes and their possessions the night before and never knew all they have worked for was to be taken from them the following morning; neither did the surviving ones know that the following day they would be made homeless. Adding to this thought I asked, where is the technology of civilization and the control we so pride ourselves to have?

We continue to be reminded that we are nothing on this earth, but for some unknown reason humanity continues with empty vain glories of self-worth pretending that we are something. Let me interject here that it is okay to think that we are something or somebody, because we are made in the image of God. At the same breath we must never fail to know that in the image of the One whom we are made, should never be mean that we are now God. We are nothing without Him in our lives. Before this sad tragedy I am sure there were a few who wagged their finger to say there is no God, but found themselves calling on God to save there lives and some may have been saved. This situation may be for them the demonstration that indeed there is God, and believers from now on they will be, or may become.

There are those who may have all along believed in God and have lost all their belongings, their homes, and their loved ones. And the time may be for some or the few, a time to ask the question where was God? On either side of this, let me say that God is in the midst of it all. He is the creator of the universe and He is the God who is always there and in control. We are workers of instrumentation for His glory. It is well put in Ephesians 2:10, "For we are His workmanship, created in Christ Jesus for good works, Which God prepared beforehand so that we would walk in them." This means that God empowers us for the work of salvation. God uses every situation for His purposes. Hard as it is we must find strength and hope in God and look forward to a future with His promise that will always be there for us. Our pains and grief are natural; are we supposed to mourn yes, but we must never fail in knowing that all belonged to God first, and that includes possessions of life and our children before we had them.

Equally as we grieve, God grieves most. I have seen and heard of parents who have become angry at God for allowing their children or loved ones to die. If I can offer this piece of advice, we cannot allow ourselves to grow to that point of being angry at God where we become sinful in our anger. God is the life-giver and the taker of life; the One that wounds and the One that heals according to Deuteronomy 32:39. We cannot afford to be angry at the One whose hands our life is dependent on. And even in this state of affairs of loosing loved ones, I have known people who are Christians walk away from their faith because of their disappointment. Now, how much knowledge of the Word of God was theirs I do not know, but one thing is certain that a good acceptance of the Word of Truth equips our understanding in this area for the times of hurts and the times of pain.

It is certain that a clear perceptive of our place concerning our relationship with God becomes important and somehow understood if we are willing to know that He is God and we are not. We are His subjects for His works and good purposes. Yes, truly a loving Father He is, but we must at all times be interfaced with the reality in our interaction that who we are does not give us the right to dishonor God. We cannot question God's sovereignty. Our question must no more or less be for the purposes of clarity with a heart of obedience on our part. God retains the right in every way to do as He pleases with us; to question God and His authority and be angry where some have actually hated God and walk away from faith, is to think too much of one.

Another side in the writing of this chapter is for me to ask the reader here to think for a moment how much ownership we exert in the places we call our homes and our cars. Do we not totally come and go as we please in them? Do we not place things and rearrange things as we please in them? Why, because they are ours. So also, do we belong to our maker who is God? Again, thinking otherwise is of the fallen state of mind called pride. There is one before us called Satan, and that was his problem. The scripture makes this clear in the writing of Apostle Paul stating, "But indeed, O man, who are you to reply against God? Will the thing formed say to him who formed it, why have you made me like this? Does not the potter have power over the clay, from the same lump to make one vessel for honor and another for dishonor? (Romans 9:20-21)." God has the sovereign right blessed saints to curse pain if He chooses, even death. There are those reading who might not know this that the same God of love is the same God in death, the same God of thorn is the same God of roses, and by the way, even the roses themselves carry their thorn on the stems even while the beautiful rose glows. Yes, some might read this and say well that is easy for you to say, but trust and know that it is this understanding that has helped me in the time of my own bereavements. You must have the knowledge of His WORD, and the understandings of His power as God the Only Sovereign One.

As humans our emotions are raw in every way possible. The knowledge of the Word can never take away our deep hurts and pains immediately; however there is no other healing power that can bring us to that place of accepting what we will confront us and the path of finding peace, than the Word of Truth. So let us learn to never say *never* of what we will never do or where we will never go, because God might just allow those forbidden situations, forgotten people or places, to be our Achilles heel.

Chapter 11

Attitudes and Rebellious Questions of "Why Should I?"

So many times in life and in the ministry I have confronted people who will say what they will never do, or places they will never go, or they will make a statement as to why they refuse to do certain things, even when the Bible is clear about those things. Most of all is their rebellious questions of "why should I?" Yet in this question the Word of the Lord is embossed as to why they should, but they reject it. One example of such character is the Biblical account of a man called Jonah. Jonah could not be any more vagrantly disobedient to God and His commandments.

The Bible tells us that Jonah was a man of God, a prophet who allowed his cultural influence to overshadow the ways of God. I write this because he is called a nationalist. A nationalist is by definition a separatist, pro-culture and pro-self-government. Jonah loved his people more than he loved God. In the church today there are too many Jonahs' who are chosen by God like Jonah was, but their pride is not about God and the gospel, it is about their culture and nationalism. These men and women are those with attitudes and are rebellious; they are the ones who ask the question, "Why should I?" This stock has no allegiance to God. Their allegiance is to their culture and their national flag. They are simply not committed to the church, which by the way in case any missed the understanding of what the church is, God is the church. Sometimes I have been in places called churches where they pledge allegiance to their earthly nation's flag before their Christian allegiance. I have nothing against any being proud of their culture and their national flag but when that comes before God, that becomes a problem for me personally... and the community of our LORD and Savior, called the church. You might ask why Apostle Uche? Simply put; no nation of the earth or culture should be placed above God and His church in my view.

These Jonahs' of the church are a problem to the church because they walk in disobedience of the commandments of God. The communities suffer because where the people in the communities walk and live in darkness the community degenerates in moral order and therefore lack peace which is the glue that holds a community. Jonah disobeyed God and God's commandment which was for him the call to go to the people of Nineveh whom he thought were culturally less than his own. He believed that God was the God of His own kind and not of those people, and oh boy, or girl' was he wrong. God is LORD of all, the creator of all whose mercy is for the people including the people of Nineveh, not just the people of Israel. There are these pervasive attitudes among some in the body of Christ that think God is theirs, for their culture. They think they have it all figured-out, but this is nothing more than ignorance on their part of who our God is.

These Jonahs' are the rebels in the churches. Some of them are the heads of the denominations. A great many of these Jonahs' are in the seminaries and most are heads of these institutions, and some are the sideline intellectuals. Some of these people hold seminary degrees and other degrees but for them it's no more about God. It is about their nationalistic agendas and the hegemonic position and predisposition. It is not for them about teaching the truth; it is about bending the truth thereby making Christianity a Western, Eastern, Northern, or Southern ideological thinking or perspective which is all that matters to them. May I say rather that Christianity again, is about God! These Jonahs' seem to forget that just as there were people from where Abraham came before his becoming Jewish; Christianity was never theirs to begin with. It was not part of their culture before they came to it; it is and will be about God and His Truth. God could have chosen any nation on earth but as it pleased Him choosing Abraham was really God reminding humanity that He is God of all because He took him from one non-Jewish stock to birth another (a Jewish stock) using them to tell His story on earth for the rest of us. If we believe the Divine birth of Christ, we should stop for a moment as well and ask the question, was there another reason behind Jesus Christ not being born of the natural conception? Other than Him being without sin, is there something more to it. Can we think deeper to see God in Jesus as God showing us He is the Father of all?

My brothers and sisters in Christ Jesus, when you are nationalistic as Jonah was you run the risk of not being an impartial person in all your ways. That was exactly the problem with Jonah; and as Jonah you are bound to be disobedient to the commandment of God as he was. Your judgment in hiring in ministry, in association, and fellowship will no longer be God focused and Christ centered. You are now led by the forces of the earthly realm that brings about division, subjugation, hate and pride, all not of God. To be of God is to be of no persuasion; what do I mean? To claim to be a Christian as an individual or of a Christian university, college, and seminary, or church and your persuasion is of the western, eastern, northern, and southern persuasions. You might just call yourself a political arm of a movement and not truly a Christian institution. Any persuasion other than biblical persuasions focused on God and His ways, is a joke.

God made a fool out of Jonah with his bias against the people of Nineveh by showing His mercy to the people of Nineveh, which Jonah never thought they deserved as a people. To see the action of God is to be reminded of the scripture in Proverbs 21:2-3, "Every man's way is right in his own eyes; But the LORD weighs the hearts. To do righteousness and justice is desired by the Lord more than sacrifice." This is important for us as Christians. We must remember that no matter what humanity feels, no matter the cause, no sacrifice for any earthly nation should be greater than the cause of truth, righteousness, and justice always should be the focus. It does not mean we deny the truth because that will be denying God. Jonah could not see anything good about the Ninevites. In his own human concept they were all hopelessness and doomed to destruction. Jonah and his anger in chapter 4 of the book of Jonah, revealed his perception and his misjudgment of God. Jonah 4:2-3 states, "So he prayed to the Lord, and said, "Ah, LORD, was not this what I said when I was still in my country? Therefore I fled previously to Tarshish; for I know that you are gracious and merciful God, slow to anger and abundant in loving kindness, one who relents from doing harm. Therefore now, O LORD, please take my life from me, for it is better for me to die than to live!" Jonah's cry of self-pity is pathetic. Why? Because his vision of people not worthy was reversed by the mercies of God after the Ninevites repented. Too many Jonahs' are found in the churches, or institutions, who write people off too quickly. The acknowledgement of one for them must be from their thwarted view of a particular race, and their myopic understanding of what they have summed-up to be of God. But they forget that God is the only one who determines when and how the end comes.

To ignore who the Lord is and continue to allow people who are lukewarm at best and not controlled by the spirit of God, can stir up confusion and defeat the work of ministry. I recently spoke to a young lady who told me that to give alms to a person in-need must mean that they have no cell phone or cable in their home. I listened and I said is that right? Now this person is in a church where the head of the church is known to be well-off, with fleets of expensive cars, probably multi-million dollar home, or homes, and if the truth be told she probably writes him a check for his care. And let me say that there is nothing wrong with that in any way because 1Corinthians 9:9-12 states, "YOU SHALL NOT MUZZLE THE OX WHILE HE is THRESHING." We are not to muzzle the mouth of those that speak into our lives. But when I got through thinking of what she said I asked myself where this excuse of hers in the bible is? Is what she is saying simply that if I do not like you I won't give? How could one give to the one very affluent, and justify her actions not to give to the needy because they have a cell phone. Why would people be so blatant that they find it easy to violate God's laws by writing-off their fellow human beings based on how they feel or what they have determined in their own perception and how they assume what the outcome of life should be, this is sad and pitiful?

May we learn to walk always in obedience to God's commandment no matter our discomfort. Amen.

Chapter 12

+———————————————————————

Why Not Our Cultural Way?

This chapter is about why it is dangerous to put too much significance on cultures instead of our Christian faith. In our present time a majority of the colleges and seminaries are on the train of cultural-context. What this means is that evangelism should be done in the context of the culture that is being evangelized. In the western thinking cultural context is a way to correct mistakes of the past style of evangelism. In the past natives were denied the right to worship God in the culture they were familiar with. The growth of Islamic inroads to the entire North Africa and the other parts of Africa has been somewhat the result of this method of evangelism, they claim. Because Islam allowed the natives to keep to what they were familiar with, i.e. multiple marriages, this made it easier for them to embrace the Islamic faith instead of Christianity. And the truth is that they may be right in some ways of this thinking. However, the danger with this thinking is the unintended consequences which follow this same idea.

There are many who seem to think that their culture should be placed ahead of the instructions of the bible. Some are naively elevating their culture above the ways God. While I do not write to forsake the uniformity of worship, when there is transportation of cultural forms which are held higher than what is biblically practiced, I think we run the risk of denying God and placing the ways of man higher. I know the question that some might be thinking of right now is, what are you talking about? Is the Bible not written around the

Jewish culture? You may be right to a point but let us read on. More about why I think along this line will be discussed later in this chapter but for now I will focus for a moment on why I think that our cultural way may not be the answer.

Part of the problem with this question of *"why not our cultural way"* is how it is asked. Some aspects of the cultures of people round the world are beautiful and good. Those cultures that enhance life, promote righteousness and justice are cultures to be maintained, but not all things about all cultures; some are not good. And this is where the nationalistic minded run into trouble in their thinking which often is contrary to the ways of God. Most earthly violence of humanity against their fellow human kind, prior and in our present age, is centered on cultural differences. They are quite intriguing in a sense because there is always the thinking that a particular culture is better than the other. Countless lives have been lost over cultural differences of opinion and counter opinions. The ethnocentric views have divided people across the world because of one culture elevating itself against others. Which now brings me to ask what culture is really? Culture for me in simple definition is how a particular segment or a population or group of people act or do things. The dictionary gives this definition, "Improvement of the mind, manners, etc., development by special training or care, the skills, arts, etc., of a given people in a given period; civilization." Here the interpretation must be made clear that culture is a humanity formulated opinion of how to do things, whether of arts or in care, it is the form of how those before us handled things in a given time and situation. Human beings are born into cultures; they are not born with a culture. It is only as we grow in a given region or place that we learn what is practiced or how things are done; it is in this setting that what is called culture is formed or are formed.

As one moves to another region one is influenced with the training of how things are done and a different set of training is learned and this becomes that ones culture. So, we can correctly state that environment is what shapes and influences our behaviors and this is what we call culture. We therefore can conclude that no one on earth

70

can state that they are one-hundred percent of any culture. We are in a sense not one complete whole, but a part of various particular cultures at any given moment. We are rather a byproduct of each other in forms of doing things and living. I love some of my culture and I am proud of some my culture, but not all of them. For what is considered my culture may not really be my culture but a borrowed way of living. For me at this stage to claim that my culture is perfect in its way would be crazy and no culture is. I have lived long enough to see people blinded by their culture and the cost associated with that ignorance. I have seen things in my culture that are un-objective and unfair, sexiest in practice, and destructive to families yet they are claimed to be the culture, 'this is the way things are done here they claim.' Sadly, often I hear people state, "this is the way we do things here, or this is our culture." Good. And I am for a culture that is "Right" and "Just" in every sense of the word but not when that culture is wrong and catastrophic in the practice of living; there ought to be a reevaluation. There are things that certain cultures have done or ways they are doing things in the various cultures of the world that if we are honest and not closed-minded in our thinking, readily we will admit that what was done the way it was done has been proven wrong, or is not right.

To deny this for any is to be closed- minded, dead in growth, fostering corruption, and bound in conflict within selves and with others. There are things in all cultures of this earth that are not good. Why? Because these cultures are practices of those before us, practiced by human beings, and humanity is weighed down with weakness, wickedness and biased. Because of our imperfection no culture therefore can claim perfection in essence. I have noticed in my reading there is the claim that Christianity is of the Jewish culture. Is it really? Based on what culture might I ask? Yes, we know that God used this part of the culture to tell His story on earth but can we for the position of certainty claim that all the practices are Jewish? To begin with Abraham was not Jewish. He was from Ur of the Chaldeans as we read in Genesis 12. God called him to Egypt, and after years had gone by the Jews became enslaved for four hundred years in Egypt.

There had to have been many of these other cultural ways which they absorbed. The Egyptians themselves were influenced by the Nubians for hundreds of years, with four generations of Jews born of these different cultural ways of living and doing things. Is it possible the cultures could have intermingled? Other cultural influences much, much, later lays hold from the Assyrians, Babylonians, Greeks, and the Romans. Can we for sure with assurance make the claim that Christianity is of a particular culture?

Why not our cultural way? And why I believe it should not be placed before our God of the Holy Bible is because God is the creator of all things and the Bible states in Genesis 1:1-2, "In the beginning God created the heavens and the earth. The earth was formless and void." What can be understood here is that there was no creation, no humanity in practice of any culture that ever existed before God and His creation. I know that there are those who do not believe in the created account of the Bible. Let's for a moment believe in their hypothesis that humanity came from the tree in the forest, or that a huge stone fell out of nowhere. That tree and that stone that fell must have been created or made before it even came into existence. To us as believers, when all the scientific debate and hypothesis and atheistic beliefs in their pursuit of exercise are finished, the logical and sensible answer is that God created everything before what was created came into existence.

A place that is void and without form has no substance or matter to derive, nor any possibility of being formed without God. We move on to the reading of the scripture in John 1:1-5, "In the beginning was the Word, (describing Jesus who is God) the Word was with God, and the Word was God. He was in the beginning with God. All things came into being through Him, and apart from Him nothing came into being that has come into being." There is no other explanation that makes mute the argument of anyone who thinks that culture should be placed ahead of the God of the Bible and His worship, than these two passages of the Bible. In my own Nigerian culture, if not the entirety of Africa, there is no misunderstanding of who God is. He is known as the creator of all, the sovereign God, the creator of heaven and earth. He is God whose sovereignty does not end. Whether they are Christians or not, the central bond is that there is God who is the holder of life and the universe. He is the God that is above all other gods. Now, I do know that there are some even in the country of my birth who would like to make claim that in their culture their god was or is the creator; and my answer to that thinking will be, 'really?'

Surprisingly there are those who rise to make these kinds of assertions. For them the tendency is to extol their cultural forms or ways over God is hard for me to fathom. They are either non-believers unsure of their God, or they are performers of forms in Christianity. Sometimes I have run into people who are quick to claim that Christianity is not their culture. It is an age old argument of ignorance because they have no understanding of their history or that of Christianity. A majority of this camp are nationalist minded individuals who are blind and see nothing else except their ways. Most are ethnocentric which means that their culture is the only earthly viable culture superior against all other, which is nonsense and empty of any substance for argument. A year or two ago while in a Los Angeles restaurant, I was introduced to a man I had never met in my life. He was an attorney as I was told by the young man that I was with called Okey, who introduced me as his pastor. Without any effort on my part to evangelize him he felt the liberty to insult me with his argument that my faith was borrowed and that I did not know what I was worshiping. I felt so sorry for him because he thought being an attorney meant that he knew what he was talking about having obtained a certain intellectual pride. Even so I knew he was misguided in his own arrogance, blind and lost in his foolish pride. People like this man need to be informed if they are willing to hear and learn. But to continuously look foolish by speaking in ignorance does not speak well of one who is an attorney in my estimation. Yet there are these pockets of people without depth out there who like to debate on issues they have no knowledge of, nor expertise. But it is nothing but the pride of humanity in their 'falseness.'

Our cultures when they run contrary to the ways of God, must take a bow. Jesus Christ confronted the Pharisees and the rabbinical scholars who were woven in their culture as the outfit post for the things of God. He not only condemned them for their behaviors, He challenged them to deviate from their ways that were not the ways of the Father.

Issues of culture and the cultural superiority are problematic in our times. Culture and superiority of it has been responsible for prejudice against others, racism, bigotry, and segregation; because a particular group or people believe there is something inherent in their being that cannot be found in others. So the need to seek and isolate becomes a desire which is sickening and amoral.

Tribalism which is ethnic or clannish is also from this place of belief that 'my culture is better' and so the people I must associate with and the church I go to must be the one with people like me. But is this of God? Or is it the corruption of human beings and their confused state of presence. In my previous book I may have addressed this issue and somewhere if you recall in this book I said that where there is segregation and racism with its ugly head raised, that place is not the house of God but of gods; because it is not the character of the one true God. In page 64 of Dr. Martin Luther King, Jr., *Strength to Love*, King Writes, "I say so-called Negro church because ideally there can be no Negro or white church." This was while Dr. King discussed the negligence of the church especially that of the Negro community in his time.

But where is God in this and what is God saying? God remains God and transcends all the differences we as people see and feel. I recall in reading through the Bible, that only in one chapter was there anything close to racism which occurred by the hand of Aaron and Miriam. This was in Numbers 12:1 that states, "Then Miriam and Aaron spoke against Moses because of the Cushite (Ethiopian or part of the present Sudan) woman whom he had married (for he had married a Cushite woman); and they said," Has the LORD indeed spoken only through Moses? Has He not spoken through us as well?" And the LORD heard it. (Now the man Moses was very humble, more than any man who was on the face of the earth.) Suddenly the LORD said to Moses and Aaron and to Miriam, "You three come to the tent of meeting." So the three of them came out. Then the LORD came down in a pillar of cloud and stood at the doorway of the tent, and He called Aaron and Miriam. When they had both come forward, He said, if there is a prophet among you, I, the LORD, shall make Myself known to him in a vision." Verses 9 -12 tell us how Miriam became leprous because of her opposition to Moses; not only for her challenge to Moses, both her and Aaron's racist attitude was an insult to God who is the creator of all. There is no other place in the Bible that I can recall reading anything about racism. Some might say well how about the incident in the New Testament with Peter in the book of (Acts 10) and (Galatians 2)? For me, in either case I think it was about hypocrisy; a matter of Peter finding himself in God rather than an obvious racism. There is no other place in the Bible that we read of such vile racism rather other scriptures were about idolatry not race related.

God wishes that His children at some point would grow up to become matured adults who have learned to eat solid food. We should grow to begin to see God's goodness in our fellow human beings where possible for at the end of the day we are children of the same Father. Our failure to arrive at this point means no more, no less, but a place of bondage. While out promoting my previous book, I visited with the bookstore owner who is a wonderful and sweet lady. We had a conversation about book signing and a question was asked whether a friend I had mentioned was of a particular race. I did not know the reason for the question but I think that her reasoning was pure. And just as I hesitated and was about to answer her as to what race or ethnic background my friend was, she snatched my thought by saying, "I guess you no longer see color and she added, please note that it does not matter I love all God's children." Her answer to me it appears was genuine, but my answer to her was what I have always said. I said, 'know that I see color but it no longer makes a difference." And this has been my feeling about life and how I was raised. I also added that when God has called you as His, and you come to know God and have a personal relationship with LORD, you no longer see humanity in their essence but you now learn to see God in them.

We are commanded to love one another. It is not just a saying; it is a commandment that we have been given, if we are one in Him. Our culture does not matter to God, especially when it does not glorify God and so when we prop-up this thing called culture instead of honoring God with the truth, which is what we are called to do, we have failed miserably. Let us remember this crystal clear, that until the conscience of God runs through the veins of any one who calls themselves a Christian there will not be peace in every household and every land. That conscience of God is His righteousness and justice and where these qualities are lacking we then have a problem.

May each one who calls his or herself a Christian be baptized in this conscience.

Chapter 13

Western Superiority and Cultural Cultivation of Race Domination in Christianity

I was settled on resting up with my thought process finished with the writing of the chapters of *I Hear You!...But What is God Saying?*, when the desire to address this issue of cultivation of race domination in Christianity by the West encircled my presence. As a matter of fact I had mentioned to my wife a week prior, about the prod to write on this very topic. I had to fight it off. She asked me why the reluctance. I mentioned to her my desire was staying with topics that I have addressed in the book; and also, that my aspiration was that I did not want to have the misapprehension of race and all that comes with its debates. Her next question was, is that the reason you should not write even though you felt strongly about it, and especially led in that direction? Frankly, I felt that hunger settled, but realizing that my feeling cannot be smothered the decision to write this chapter was borne out of this deep seated restlessness of sentiment.

In God and in Christianity, the Bible states that we are made in the image and the likeness of God (Gen. 1:27). We are instructed that we are all created as one people, we all have one Father, and has not one God created us all? This is the question asked in Malachi 2:10. In every attribution the desire of man and his spirituality is to seek the same creator. History teaches us that all humanity is of the same creator of the universe. Historians and those in science in their discoveries tell us that all humanity originated from Africa. In the introduction page of Thomas C. Oden, *How Africa Shaped The*

Christian Mind, Oden writes, "Decisive intellectual achievements of Christianity were explored and understood first in Africa before they were recognized in Europe, and a millennium before they found their way to North America." And so there lies the questions that I ask, why the Western Superiority and Cultivation of Race Domination in Christianity? Where is this attitude from and why is it continuing? The answer to the first part is dominance and control; Which is why the impression is given that all that is good and intellectual is European or of the West. A projected image of Africa is that of the uncivilized continent and yet, this is where all civilization has been known to have started. Hitherto in a strange way nothing of this civilization had its root out of Africa, at least that is what a majority of the entire world has been led to believe. Africa, where God and the stories of His encounter with His people are here found center stage. Still Christianity could not have begun in Africa, they say, or even the remote sensibility that the theological minds that were responsible for the teachings of Christianity were Africans. *This desire to control will cause the West to use race to subjugate the truth of history* and change the course to historical falsehood in following the agendas of a few clever theologians of the 1800 and 1900 European persuasions. Sad to say, that this immense falsehood is perpetuated up to this moment.

Writing in chapter 12 of this book, I addressed somewhat what I found of race related behavior which was not pleasing to God in the Bible. As I discussed in that chapter God dealt with it in a manner that left no uncertainty of His intolerance. God would allow the punishment for the consequences to this evil behavior and reminding us that such can not be found in God. I also stated in that chapter that there was nowhere in the Bible where the issue of race raised its ugly head; rather all that God spoke against was in reference to idolatry. To see this mind-set in the Western world with the attitude that all that is Christianity is about the West is a claim that is disgraceful, shameful, and very, very, un-Godly. God as the Creator of all must be represented in truth by Christians whether in our seminaries and our churches.

This assignment in our institutions must be what is Biblical and history courses in our schools must be taught with accuracy rather than the pretense of medieval history as the curators of Christianity and its history; this is indeed deceiving. I as a product of western educated person, have asked and wondered why in my days in the seminary much of the great theologians in the first, second, and third century were not properly taught. I have asked why more classes were not devoted to their time in history. I recall that in one of those classical evasive answers, the explanation was that their time in history was far removed from our present time. But this answer never made sense given that to teach about Jesus Christ and the original apostles was alright and which should be. I therefore, saw no credible thought to jump over into the medieval reformation without those minds that shaped Christianity and the accurate mention of their roles, and places of origin. To me this is a disservice to the informed minds.

In my reading and research all indications was that not teaching much of these early theologians was calculative and of a race based dominance attitude. The sway that Christianity has everything to do with the West and not at all with the Africans is all that mattered. Because these early theologians were predominantly Africans they may not have been the ideal information for the western-pride of education. Looking back, every effort has been made to cover up true history of those great Africans and the perpetuation of the Africa as the unenlightened continent as the normative.

As an African who has lived in the West, my associations with my brothers and sisters of the Christian faith have been met with the attitude that they own Christianity, those things about God, and the church. This was in their mind and for them it was teaching me about Christianity. This unsettling attitude of superiority in Christianity among many westerners is a feeling that says, 'we got it, you do not'. The behavior can be seen with even the most casual relationship. And while we all can and do have things to teach each other, this attitude often has been presented with this uncanny attitude of belief that Christianity is of the West. But this is not true in anyway, as Oden states,

> "It could show in more detail how Western penitential practice was profoundly shaped by Opatus of Melvis, and the teaching of justification by Marius Victorinus, it could track the influences of Africans like Minucius Felix on apologetics, of Lactantius on universal history, of Primasius on a apocalyptic interpretation, of Athanatius on civil disobedience, of Cyprian on ecclesiology, of Tertullian on theology method, of women saints like Pertua and Felicitas on eschatology courage and of Augustine on practically everything that would later be considered quintessential European."

All these people were Africans who handed to us the dogma. To read this load of history would require reading more of the book by Oden. Most Westerners have the tendencies not to associate Augustine, Origen, Alexander, Felix, etc., as Africans because they were based or influenced by the West, according to their frivolous claim. This argument is nonsense and baseless. It would mean that I as Apostle Uche, am no longer an African because I have lived in the west and have had western education. I was born and raised as an African long before my migration to the west. My early formative education was from Africa and forever I will be known as an African. These past great theologians were born Africans, rose as Africans before their migration, and they were no less Africans than I will ever be. Again, it is nothing but prejudices to make any charge that they are not genuine Africans.

All through the church whether protestant or Catholic Church (universal church), in reading what we see is these pervasive attitudes of dominance. The Catholic has this perverted control by dominance in allotting more catholic bishops to Europe even though Europe is the smallest continent with dwindling number of believers. Yet, in

Latin America and Africa with a higher growth of believers they are assigned less bishops. What could be the reason for these except that it is about the power to influence who is elected as Pope; since the bishops are the ones entrusted to elect the Pope. In most part of the world history presently there is not much knowledge of the past history of three *African* popes.

Here is a true story I experienced with fellow students while at Fuller Theological Seminary. A conversation was centered on the Catholic Church and in this discussion I brought up the fact that there had been three African Popes. Most of the students were shocked, and it was scene seen their eyes rolling-out of their heads; they thought I was crazy. They asked me as to evidence to this truth. The professor stood and was smiling as he observed this jolt of reality and the shock of information. As the debate raged I then asked them to immediately search on Google and then it was proven that I was right. One of the students was visibly angry and asked, focusing on the professor, "Why are such truths hidden and why did I have to learn about it in this form?" The questions went further as he asked, "What kind of education we are receiving when the truth is not taught." Then the professor's answer was that, "he had known that I was right." This is the problem my dear brothers and sisters in faith. Yet not in the last one-thousand five-hundred years or more had there been any African elected Pope of the Catholic Church. Even with all the outward placate of red robes and high moral spirituality of exhibition, politics in the church have taken front seat to spiritual truths with prejudice at its core; that which is of God is falsely coveted as the European brand.

The church needs to look inward if it is to make progress and heal itself of this cancerous disease of racism. Recently, the Southern Baptists made history in electing their first leader who is of non-European decent but an African American. While we commend this effort they can not stop there, they should continue on the path of asking the hard questions propelled by *what is of God* in our policies and how can we reflect Him as a church denomination. Those entrenched structures that have been discriminatory and repressive and un-Godly must be torn down and permanently destroyed in order to reflect and please God. Every other denominations must exorcise this demon in their midst. God is not pleased with this destructive divide within His church. To see denominations run towards acceptance of the world by embracing sin rather than justice and righteousness that glorifies God, is an absurdity that must be expelled.

I also write to those denominations that may have found themselves outside the main denominations of the first establishment; that while your effort is commendable of having your voice heard and recognized you too must come clean to God with a clean hand in making sure that God is pleased. When a great American called-out by God and used for the instrumentation of change in this great nation, and the church spoke, he spoke with revelations as to be expected by one led of God because he spoke with conviction in addressing the ills in the society. In few of the writings of Dr. Martin Luther King Jr. that I have been privileged to read he was a man of peace he did not stand for Injustice, he was a man who stood for Justice, he did not stand for Unrighteousness; he stood for Righteousness for all. Dr. Martin Luther King Jr. never stood for man's kingdom he stood for the kingdom that reflected God and His kingdom which abhorred sin and the sinful world of humanity. Dr. King was a man used of God before his time. He preached to the nation and the church about the understanding of oneness.

In my last book and in this one, I have been calling the church to know that if we are to be the church of God's Truth, God must be our bearer as a witness of who we are and stand for. The seminaries and the colleges that teach on God and Christianity must stand as a beacon of the Word of God. In teaching they must be charged to teach the accurate church history and not be a conduit of a political propaganda of humanity and her fallen state. They must not close their eyes else it bears naked their callous disregard for truth, and defames the obligatory responsibilities of their position. They must be willing to teach that indeed Africa brought Christianity to Europe before Europe stamped Christianity, 'made in Europe or the West' and back to Africa. The church in the West should at this point in history realize that it no longer has a cover-up on truth that will sustain itself, but the truth about the world and her history must be spoken clearly and without the barricade of line drawn by color. There has been a segment of the population that for too long been quiet; they are no longer willing to be silent. Whether it is in Africa, Asia, Latin America or Australia the young minds are asking questions that were never asked before, searching for answers that can not be quenched but the truth that needs to be told unadulterated.

God in creating different races did not ask us to be separate but united as one. He repeatedly warned us to be *one* because He is one. The church in the West and around the world must therefore strive towards the one goal of commonality and stand with God if it is to be the church of God.

Chapter 14

About Giving -Why Should I Give or Tithe?

Giving is the act of making a gift, making donations. It is to present something to someone else. God gave to us the gift of the entire world, and to humanity He gave dominion over all created things on earth. God also gave us the greatest gift of all; His only begotten Son for whosoever believes in Him will have eternal life. He presented Jesus Christ to us as a gift for the salvation of mankind. So from the beginning God has shown to us what giving is.

Why should I give or tithe to the church? This is a good question and if you are one of those reading this book and you have been asking this question, you are well within your giving right to ask. Did you just read that! 'Your giving right' also freely given to you. Simply, the answer is "Yes," you are supposed to Give. But your question will be answered on two fronts. First, you give because God has unequivocally commanded us to give to His church and to our fellow mankind. Giving is an outward sign of an inward conviction. Tithes and offerings are necessary to carry out the mission of the church. Secondly, we give to each other because there is more joy in giving than in receiving.

The first example of what giving means to God begins in Genesis 4:3-4, "So it came about in the course of time that Cain brought an offering to the Lord of the fruit of the ground. Abel, on his part also brought of the firstlings of his flock and of their fat portions. And the LORD had regard for Abel and for his offering; but for Cain and for his offering He had no regard." The moral to this story was that Abel came to God presenting his best offering but the greatest meaning is the joy with which he gave to God and his willingness to give his best. That heart of zealousness of honor to God in obedience caused God's acceptance of Abel's gift over that of his brother. Cain gave not the best but what he determined was convenient to let go. Cain was not about honoring God with a pure heart and his best. Hebrews 11: 4 tells us that it was by faith that Abel gave to God a better sacrifice and the testimony is that he was righteous (upright and in good standing with God). Abel in an act of faith gave out his best to glorify God. God has from the beginning established for us the role and the example in giving. So the idea that it is the thought that counts, not what is given, does not really make sense especially when selfishness is behind the cheap and inadequate gift. That folks frown at giving whether to the church or to their follow human beings, is crazy and irrational.

It is nothing but selfishness that leads any one individual to hold their hands closed when they have the ability to give a good gift. An example of an unselfish giving is given to us by Jesus in Luke 6:38, "Give and it will be given to you: *good measure, pressed down, shaken together, and running over will be put into your bosom. For with the same measure that you use, it will be measured back to you." Here Jesus explains that out of the selfish and conniving motive that one gives, one will receive. These are the foundations of giving established for us by God first, and then Jesus. But this is the reason also why there are many who give to the less fortunate among us. Giving is an innate desire in us. Whether it is seeking to know God or doing those things out of the desires of our heart, all good desires He alone has placed in us. The people who are less selfish, whether poor or the rich, and those with popularity who give, did not just wake up and decide it is what they are going to do in their own strength. They do it because it is a desire put in us to be fulfilled. When giving hearts give, their soul prospers not merely by seeing the expression that comes from those receiving the blessings, but also because they are reflecting the love of their creator. It is such with a wonderful feeling and a great joy when blessings of giving are bestowed one another.

I do not know about others or those who do not feel the warmth whether in giving or even in receiving. But one thing is certain for me, that there is a rewarding and overwhelming sense of pleasure when I see the smile on the faces of others as I am used as a blessing in people's lives. Now, if you are accepting Jesus and God as one, which is what we believe in our faith and the foundation of Christian teaching, then God has spoken and if He has spoken, less divide we will find in the commandment which was given in the Old Testament, rather it will be seen as a continuum. The meaning of what Jesus was saying in Luke 6 speaks to the gains that one gets when one gives unselfishly. This gain occurs when the content in the measuring cup is pressed, or compressed down, and the final output of the measure is greater than a regular measure of a cup not shaken down, pressed, or pushed down. There are blessings in giving to others and that blessing comes from God to us. But a selfish heart gives without a pure heart. These hearts that give deceivingly receive the reward of either being rejected or equally of the same measure.

Regarding the tithing, for generations there have been raging debates over whether tithing is required in our time or a law of the past not presently applicable, especially to the New Testament era to those who are proponents of such thought. Let me be bold to state that part of these debates is because there are those Christians among us who see the divide between God and Jesus. These camps of thought are the same who see the difference in the Old Testament and the New Testament. Some have even gone as far as having what they call the New Testament churches where for some most of their teachings are restricted to the Gospels or the New Testament scriptures. But the truth must be told that hardly can we find a scripture in the New Testaments whose brothers and sisters in scripture are not found or traced back into the Old Testament.

And so, for me the New Testament is incomplete without the Old Testament because the foundations of that which we call the New Testament spoken in the new languages are mostly if not all, traced in direct reference from the Old. In the Bible as we journey through the chapters on tithing it begins from Genesis 14:20. In Genesis 28:22

it states, "This stone, which I have set up as a pillar, will be God's house, and all that you give me I will surely give a tenth to You." This was Jacob committing to God the tithe.

Other chapters will follow such as in Exodus 23:19, "You shall bring the choice first fruits of your soil into the house of the LORD your God." Who are the "You" here? The children of Israel and the present children of Israel are who? The church and God's people today! Remember that all that was done with those of the past was to show us the road to who God is and how we are to conduct ourselves in our time, which is the same with New Testament. And so, what we see here is the same experience of God with Cain and Abel repeated. God requires our best and in our period of living money substitutes crops since we are no longer in the agrarian era. In Exodus 34:26 the command appears again and this time it reads "first fruits of your soil." I stated in a previous chapter how God established and commanded that the Levites were to receive no inheritance and decreed that the rest of the eleven tribes are to contribute to their well-being. I did mention that the present day priests or pastors or ministers of the gospel are to be paid, for it was in this light that the Bible declares that out of the table which a man or woman of God preaches, there they must eat from.

Here we see the commandment of God regarding tithing in Leviticus 27:30, "Thus all the tithe of the land, of the seed of the land or of the fruit of the tree, is the Lord's; it is holy to the LORD." In line with this order of tithing the Lord said to Moses in Numbers 18:25, "Moreover, you shall speak to the Levites and say to them, 'When you take from the sons of Israel the tithe which I have given you from them for your inheritance, then you shall present an offering from it to the LORD, a tithe of the tithe." We are not only commanded to tithe to the priests, Apostles, Prophets, Evangelist, Pastors, teachers of the gospel; but when they are blessed with an offerings or seeds sowed into their hands they are commanded to sow back into the hand of God from that which He has blessed them through His obedient saints.

While we are on the subject of tithe of the tithe by the priest, it will be worthy to mention that these warnings from God were directed to the leaders of the church called the priests or the pastors. The warning was and is, to those who are living a lie, not living according to the commandment of God as He has commanded us to live and this is in Malachi 1:6, "A son honors his father, and a servant his master. Then if I am a father, where is My honor? And if I am a master, where is My respect?' This is how serious the commandment of God in tithing and giving to His house is seen. This warning is to the leaders of the house of God to follow strictly in obedience the ordinance of sacrificial giving. The same trend of warning can be read in (Malachi 2:1-4), "and now this commandment is for you, O priest. If you do not listen, and if you do not take to heart to give honor to my name," says the LORD of hosts, "then I will curse your blessings; and indeed I have cursed them already; because you are not taking it to heart. Behold, I am going to rebuke your offspring, and I will spread refuse on your faces, the refuse of your feasts; and you will be taken away with it. Then you will know that I have sent this commandment to you, that My covenant may continue with Levi," says the Lord of hosts." This is the warning to the priest in the Old Testament to wake them up from their complacency; their lack of giving glory to God brings the curse not only on material blessings but in all aspects of God's graciousness. This curse of disobedience some might say is only to the Levi, and the Old Testament priests. But if we accept that it is God at work, as He worked with those before us, we know that this is His example for us. Then the tithing in their time is present in our age (which I believe it is). Therefore, the warning is equally applicable to the present priests, the pastors, and the saints of God in our time.

(Deuteronomy 14: 22), "You shall surely tithe all the produce from what you sow, which comes out of the field every year." Meaning you shall tithe from your salary, investment gains, your inheritance, any kinds of monies that you receive from other sources; it does not matter the person that gave it to you or whether he or she paid taxes on it, once it is transferred from one hand to another with gains - you tithe. Every year, month, weekly as you are paid, you are commanded to tithe. The tithing instruction continued as a commandment of God from that time forward. In Nehemiah 10 the instruction to the priests who are ministering in the house our God is that they are to receive the tithe, and the tithe of the tithe also to the house God. There are some additional scriptures in the Bible from 2 Chronicle 31: 5-6, to Amos 4:4, Ezek. 45:11, and 1 Samuel 8:15, 17; these are all about the tithing. Incidentally, tithing did not stop after the time of Moses it had continued.

The New Testament mentions of tithing but Jesus stressed what mattered to God. Allowing the Bible to speak for itself it states in Matthew 23:23, "they neglected the weightier provisions of the law: justice and mercy and faithfulness; but these are the things you should have done without neglecting the others." Jesus Christ never condemned tithing but reminded the Pharisees of the importance of what mattered most to God centering on His Love. In Hebrews 7:6-9 we are reminded of the tithing of Abraham to Melchizedek and that Abraham not only paid his tithing, he blessed him. And the same chapter talks about the authority which was invested to the priest by the Mosaic Law to collect the tithe. The people of Israel honored this law not particularly the priest but they honored God and His law. In our time that is our responsibility. Apostle Paul in 1 Corinthians 16:1 establishes and directs the saints with the order of giving to the church, every week as a matter of fact, to put aside as they have prospered. That the word tithing was not used here makes it no less important, after all the same phrase "as they prospered" was used even in the Old Testament before Apostle Paul used it in his time. In Galatians 6:6-8 Apostle Paul writes of how the minister of the gospel, the one who teaches, should be blessed even in the material things; and he goes further to warn the saints that God is not mocked because God knows when they can do more and choose not to for selfish reasons and he warns on the dangers of sowing sparingly. The scripture in 2 Corinthians 8-9 does not in any way diminish nor limit tithing in the New Testament in any way possible.

The debate on this issue for so long has been for those who argue that we are in the time of grace therefore tithing is no longer required, is interesting. I did write in my previous book how grace is not a license to sin. And I also, did discuss that grace was never a new concept but has been from the beginning of time. I think that the Bible makes it clear that there is nothing new that has never been. God from the beginning of time has established the rules of how things should be. For us in our thinking of how things ought to be in this age of dispensation by discarding all that has been and invent a new way or method, is not acceptable. I know somebody reading might say, well does that mean that those draconian laws in the ancient times should be applied in our time? The answer is no, and if close attention is paid to the Bible we know that it was through man that the law of draconian rules came out of. In it the law grew to a total of 613 man made laws. These were not of God or the commandments that He gave to Moses. The law if practiced as the LORD had intended it to be there would not have been the draconian laws.

Having said this here we must hold to the truth knowing that God "changeth not;" as we are instructed, in Hebrews 13: 8. We are to grow wary of those who teach strange doctrines WANTING TO ADAPT THE WORD OF God to THEIR COMFORT LEVEL hence the scripture says that God is the same yesterday, today, and forevermore. The purpose for grace was not to nullify the commandments of GOD, it was to help us overcome, it was to show us the right way. Jesus did not walk the earth declaring that His Word is now null and void. He came to shed the light on the wrongs that mankind had chosen and that included those other laws that aggrieved His people. The scripture that is often misused and misrepresented is found in Matthew 5:17-20 but the truth here is those laws of His which were commanded and working was not to be messed with. Jesus was not giving new Laws nor was He modifying the old ones, but He was simply explaining the Law He gave to Moses; Tithing in that commandment; is enjoined in our time.

What was the purpose of tithing that was given in the Old Testament and the New Testament? It was and it is all in a commonality of purpose to honor God, equip and take care of His church, and His chosen servants. Therefore any who claim that tithing is not required in our time is wrong in their thinking and where they have used the scripture to justify this claim, they are mistaken.

Over the years there have been horrific stories of the greedy bunch that are in the ministry they have abused the call of God in their lives. Some not called at all have walked away from their calling, and money grabbing and money grubbing has become their caller. These people are really no longer serving God they are now serving their self-interest and their cronies that they run along with. It is all about money. These are the people who will tell you that God told them that if you sow a seed for certain amount, God will bless you in the manner of the same equal amount of seed sowed. While I cannot defend these kinds of statements or deny their claim, I know in my own spiritual work with God, He is yet to tell me to take such brazen bold steps. These kinds of claims are often scary and I would advise anyone who receives such instructions or claims to be very careful and proceed in caution. I do know that we cannot limit God nor put God in a box, but on thing I know is that God cannot be bribed by exchanging money for blessings, especially by those of questionable spiritual integrity.

My advice to those who question the tithe and giving to the church is simple, do you pay to see the Doctors, Lawyers, Psychologists, and the Psychiatrists? Why? Because of services that are provided. The churches are providing major services to God's children. Most of us do not even ask questions; it is assumed that it is okay to pay upwards of $25-$35 dollars just to knock at the doctor's door before we can even see the Doctors. Most lawyers charge consultation fees of $250-$500 dollars, and of course we have no problem writing a check for $150-$250.00 dollars to speak to a Psychologist or Psychiatrists for an hour. And this is good, but why do we find it a problem giving to the church? Is it because the culture of the churches does not demand it as these other professions? We should know that some of the servants of these churches have studied as hard as these other professions, if not more in some cases. The other point that must be made here is that it costs money to run the affairs of any church. Those comfortable chairs we make demands of in churches, the air conditioning, the electricity, maintenance of the premises, the employees that have to be paid, childcare, insurance, and the cost of the building; these are the reasons and many more that the saints of God must understand the reason to give, and give to a church abundantly.

There are those who will read *I Hear You!...But What is God Saying?*, and they might be wondering why they have been tithing because they have been waiting to see some return on their investment. This thought may be natural, but a dangerous one. We should give without compulsion, yet we should not expect that we are owed anything in return with our giving; we give to God because we are commanded to give. We give because He has given so much more to you and me. God gave His only begotten son for us all. We cannot out-give God. Our daily life existence is in His hands, and aside, all that we have belongs to Him from the beginning of time to the present and to the end to come. Can we for a moment stop and take a stock of the many blessings of God that we have taken for granted. Can we think for a second what is the most important thing for our daily life existence and possible could have been the most expensive item in life if it were sold daily, is the air that is freely given called oxygen? You might think that my thinking is extreme however thirty years ago no one thought that water would be sold. Aside from the cost we incur in purifying the water which by our own irresponsibility has become contaminated, think how water which is given to humanity freely by God has been turned into a huge business. Does anyone calculate the cost for drinking water today all over the world and wonder what it would cost if we paid for air? God has given so much to us and when we are given the opportunity to give back, it ought to be of a cheerful heart in giving. We do not give with the attitude of a quid pro quo (exchange for something) or on the thought of us holding a basket to receive at the any appointed time, but we can hope in the blessings of God because the Word of the LORD has promised us that there will be a reward.

Long ago, a young lady who was a member of our church for a while narrated her encounter with her former pastor to me. She told me how she was hurt that in moment of her need the church was unable to assist her after all the monies/tithing that she had given to the church. Further in the conversation she told me she confronted the pastor and cursed him-out; for that reason she had to leave.... she said, what purpose is there for me to give, if the church cannot help me when I need them? I listened to this sad story, coming to the knowledge of her formed understanding of what she thought was the reason to give or tithe, and then thinking for a moment that she is going to repeat the same thing to me in this church. Grant it that I do believe church as community that has the ability should help, but is this the reason to give or tithe? This young lady may not have been favored because of her motive for giving and tithing if she did tithe her reasons was wide of the mark in the first place.

We are commanded, and in obedience we all should walk in it by giving and tithing; however the reward may not come through the church, God being LORD of all could at any point bless us through many means possible. The blessings of God may not be in the form of a monetary gain, it may be through health, peace of mind, joy, trouble free family, or marriage, a good place of employment or even financial blessings, we may never know. God has called us all to walk in obedience to His commandment and it is our utmost responsibility to make sure that our lives are lived accordingly. Anything that is short of this means no more, no less, but that we are in disobedience.

Be blessed as you walk in obedience to His commandment.

Chapter 15

A Message to the Church

The chapter "*A Message to the Church*," speaks to all churches of God across the world. God is one and His body cannot be divided. Yes, there are different cultures of the world but with God all the cultures mean nothing for they are but the formulated procedure of mankind and their ways on earth. God sees His children as one regardless of race, gender, or creed, as long as they are walking in obedience to His commandments and for His glory. I know there are churches all over the world whose leaders are faithful to their calling and are striving to walk in righteousness. Then this message may not be directed to you, and if you are one of those and you happen to find yourself reading this book, I praise the God Almighty for you, and I am sure that the LORD is rejoicing for your stand for the Truth. The message to the church here is that God is mourning because His heart is broken for the church has not lived up to its responsibilities to His people and for His glory.

We have for too long sat on the sidelines and far too long we have failed in the defense of the Truth which is the Word of God which is God. There would not be Christianity as it is known today if the apostles and the early church fathers before our time sat on the sidelines praying without the actions of speaking-out and challenging the establishment that was in their time. It was because of their uncompromising stand for their belief, their fearlessness in the defense of what they believed in, their steadfastness, dedication, devotion to God against the forces of evil and oppression that a great many nations of the world and their king's even up to our present generation, enacted laws that turned countries we now know as Christian nations. These nations that call themselves Christian nations probably might not be known as such today. The ease with which some of the present church leaders are willing to compromise in the things of God and the Word of God is disgraceful and the heart of God bleeds. It begs one to ask, are these people truly called of God? To be silent when the walls are crumbling all around us is to be a party to and accepting that it is okay for the walls to fall to pieces. Not standing for what we believe, is not standing up for anything. And so, the church and its leaders must speak without any equivocation.

The saints before us not only prayed but they supported their prayer with events by their love (actions) for what they believed in. They waged war against the forces of evil. The disciples and most early fathers were quite willing to lay down their lives; they were not afraid and were not primarily interested in fame or material wealth instead they were about the business of the Father. All the disciples of Jesus except Apostle John, who lived to an old age, gave their lives as they were martyred for the gospel. Beginning with Genesis to Revelation we are called to stand and defend the Truth of the Word. In the writing of Apostle Paul he charged Timothy, his son in the ministry, with these words, "I solemnly charge you in the presence of God and of Christ Jesus, who is to judge the living and the dead, and by His kingdom: preach the word; be ready in season and out of season; reprove, rebuke, exhort, with great patience and instruction" (2 Timothy 4:1-3). As church leaders of our time, we are charged to express disapproval with immoral laws of society and how we can do this is through making our voices heard in our communities, cities, and states. We are to scold and reprimand those championing laws and rules dangerous to our nation's existence. We cannot continue to bury our heads in the sand with utter silence.

There is too much silence among the body of believers and in the church corporately. I have had it with the so-called large or mega church leaders who do nothing more than look for personal acceptance and popularity in the hands of politicians and populace. Those of you who claim to speak for God and say you are called of God, when are you going to rise from this coma and take a stand as one who is called? Do you not know that God has always used human beings on earth to do His work? And that involves the full participation of the church leaders speaking up and speaking the truth. How long is the dancing of popularity going to go on while the society around us is crumbling? God has not called us for the personal comfort but to be the agent of change in the lives of individuals and the society. Not through acquiring buildings alone is our success measured, but that of societal moral sanctity. God is asking and seeking for true servants who will no longer be silent about sin. He is looking for those not interested in the outward image of a copy Christian rather those with conviction who have fearlessness and what it takes to stand for the truth acknowledging that God is leading.

Silence in the face of evil, whether in the society as a whole or within the church, causes the wrath and indignation of God that pours out onto society and upon His people. God indeed is a consuming fire who requites it upon the heads of those in disobedience and that judgment begins with the church. God is warning whether it is in Nigeria, or the United States or other parts of the world, by asking the church, "why the silence to the moral decays in our society?" (sexual immorality), evils of oppression against the poor, crimes against widows and the widowers, the elderly, the shedding of innocent blood, the destruction of innocent lives for dishonest gains.

Those people before our time sacrificed enormously so that the work of God may prosper and people in the society saw meaning for the purpose for which they gathered. Not only did people experience the miraculous power of God, the people saw their leaders who were in full participation in the suffering that the leaders might attain the ultimate goal which was to serve God. Presently, in our time we see some so-called leaders of our churches who are afraid of dying, unwilling to sacrifice; they are unwilling to participate in night vigils or even fasting in some cases. For the leaders of our time those kinds of activities are left to those who are more in the need for the spiritual things of God. I guess their thinking may be that they the (leaders) have attained it, or so they think, yet they are lost.

Two days ago in talking to a pastor I was told a tragic story. It was about the abandonment of a church by a pastor because the number of attendees had dropped to 40 persons and the pastor decided that he had had enough and could not put up with it anymore. This to me was tragic in the sense that over and over this story is common place in our time, where so called leaders abandon their church work for a greener pasture. Not truly knowing all that was involved here; I know that in some situations the struggles of entrenched board members who make claims of church as theirs has led to some faithful preachers finding themselves frustrated where they have no other choice but to walk away. It happened to a friend of mine whom I have come to love dearly as a brother. His board decided that God's church was now theirs to rule and run as they saw fit. This well intentioned brother, who loves the LORD and labors up until this moment for the glory of the LORD, had to quit because the board did not want him to lead. They saw themselves as the heir apparent to the church- leadership instead of the shepherd. This is a common occurring event in our time especially in the United States where denominations have turned churches into democratic board rooms. It is the new trend a corporate and democratic structure introduced to the church which frankly is destroying the community of Christ we call church. This is wrong; there is no ship in the high sea that is led by more than one captain. It is either that the captain directs the traffic because he or she is leading the compass direction, or every one leads into their own direction and the ship often runs aground. When situations like these arise it is of no surprise that the frustrated shepherd will see no other choice of action than to yield to pressure by quitting.

This kind of situation is quite understandable, but too frequently too many stories of some who pack up their backs and walk out on faithful members have become common. It begs to ask what might have been their motive. Were they chosen from the start or did they choose the ministry thinking wealth and riches was the goal, and only for them to find disappointment that it is not what the work of ministry is about. While I write here with no condemnation to any who choose to resign from the ministry for other reasons than what is mentioned, however of those who abandon their vocation their behaviors I find appalling that anyone who truly loves God will ditch their love for earthly enrichment. This is why one must be called for this work in order for them to achieve the goal of serving the Lord and His people. Heartaches will indeed happen, lacks will come, sacrifice (not convenient sacrifice) will be required, feeling of disappointment will be presented and the temptation of abandonment will be tested; but guess who is your strength through it all, the God of grace.

The church is commanded to tell the truth, not water down the Word. The church is called to be a sanctified place, a Holy ground, not Broadway where everything that comes passes through. The church is called to be a Healing place not a Resting place. The church is called to be a place of Deliverance not a place of Death on arrival. The church is a place where the Captive is set free not where the Captor is kept. The church is a place of Faithfulness not Faithlessness. The church is a place of Justice and Righteousness not for Injustice and Unrighteousness. The church is a place of Hope not Hopelessness. And the church definitely ought to be a place of Sinless-ness not a place of Sinfulness. The church is supposed to be a House of Prayer, not a house Entertainment and a den of Robbers.

What is therefore the solution to this madness? As I have pointed out in chapter one, the essential requirement is to be called first and foremost. The other pertinent requirement is that those in church leadership across the globe, who are struggling, must be willing to seek help in alignment with true men and women who are walking in truth and integrity, living righteously, and faithful to their own calling. These people are to become their mentor and prayer partners with God as their anchor. I am aware that humanity and their egos can be a challenge but a true man and women of God walks in humility and are likely to accept the role of mentorship if the mentee is indeed seeking for the guidance in truth. The order in this search must not be based on the spirit of carnal desires. What I mean here, is simply that one cannot be led by the flesh in their search or else the authentic people will be mixed because the flesh attracts what the world has determined to be success. And when this is the case, what is sought for is then one with a large or mega ministry and my brothers and sisters of the faith, while in our eyes it look successful and great; it may not be for God. Again, let me be clear that there are many successful men and women with large ministries who are of great character and of integrity that possess the qualities I have listed above, and please seek them out if you are being led in that direction. But my advice here is what is important, and why it should not be focused through the eyes of the world if we want to reflect the hallmark of a successful ministry, which is centered on Jesus Christ.

The other area I dare point out in this "message to the church," is that churches for centuries have focused on the quest of knowledge but that quest with all its achievements has placed less emphasis on the Spiritual side of God and His Church. Instead the church has embarked on the intellectual pursuit and more in the acquisition of Ph.D.'s. But the more of our attainment in this area the further and weaker the church seems to have become. It challenges us to ask the question whether too much head-knowledge and reliance on that paper accreditation has caused the ineffectiveness of the church in Spiritual area of growth. Having appreciated the academics to a degree with a sense of gratitude, I am also deeply troubled by what I see as the innate problem of humanity and that is the spirit of mankind called the flesh.

It is the "I know it all attitude" that reminds me of the story in Acts. The Holy Spirit had fallen and the diverse people were heard or had spoken in tongues described as the "Wonderful works of God." The response by some in Acts 12:13, was, "They are full of new wine." Those who mocked are like the sample of many in our time and in our churches, our institutions, and our seminaries. It must be reminiscent to our churches that it was the scholarly-mindedness of the supposedly rabbinical scholars that failed them when the Messiah appeared because with their entire high educated mind they missed Him. They had so much focused on their own spiritual interpretation of their studies; where He was supposed to come from, the kind of kingdom expectation they were looking for (not God's kingdom), that they denied the Savior on appearing.

Our present church and institutions run the same risk if Jesus Christ were to appear among us in the present because of our obsession with intellectual exercise, many of us would miss Him. Maybe the world will repeat the experience of not recognizing Our Lord and Savior Jesus Christ in His coming back. God made use of the not so scholarly (ordinary men and women) in Acts 4:13, "Now when they saw the boldness of Peter and John, and perceived that they were uneducated and untrained men; they marveled. And they realized that they had been with Jesus." The church needs to learn from the foundation of our faith through the examples left to us that our exercise is an exercise of futility when the Holy Spirit is not the leading agent.

Everything about the Spiritual things of God we almost have thrown out the window. It is about the study of man, the anthropology, the Culture, the Sociology, the Psychology, (while there may be the need of these on some level) just not the Holy Spirit; that is the territory we dare not venture to (*sarcastically speaking*). In some of our institutions or Seminaries the mere act or claim of the Holy Spirit and acknowledgement calls for expulsion. Yet the sem-i-nary, according to Webster dictionary is "a school where ministers, priests, or rabbis are trained." The question then in our time must be of; trained for what? Is it in this same academic wall, where some of those teaching also question what they believe in? A place that is supposed to train future church leaders but no Bible is not ever opened in some classes nor are prayers said in most of the classes. Seminary is where much that is taught is skewed to favor a particular political perspective; where the history of some but not the historical truths of biblical history are taught. It is a place where everything that is of the church is made a mockery of in some instances, and a place not God centered.

Some might ask what in the world is he talking about, who does he think he is? There are so many men and women who are anointed and as well are educated. I have no quarrel of this assertion from anyone. My answer to these thoughts will be if that was the case we will see more leaning of the spiritual reflected in our churches, our institutions, and our seminaries of learning. We would see that in the classes taught and maybe, just maybe, those who attend will go out of these institutions into the churches with a pragmatic sense of purpose of the awareness of "the Holy Spirit." Out of these seminaries apprehensive of not living the life of sin while in these institutions, the churches, and even outside of it when they are in the world will become part of the zeal for God. What awaits us outside the walls of academia, outside the corridors of life, is too great a force that only if we are dominated by the Supernatural Power can we impact and affect lives. The battle cannot be won by men and women who are without the spiritual amour of God, but with those equipped in the knowledge and the Power of God. The word holiness and the act of holy living must become the first rule of discipline. For the church, and our institutions, to be the change agent of the Holy Spirit, they must wear the mantle of a change agent called the HOLY SPIRIT.

Conclusion

I hear you! But what is God Saying? is a book written to inform believers and God's children around the world that God welcomes our questions when we are unsure of the instruction to the message He is giving to us. On subjects and moments of uncertainty God wants us to get from Him exactitude of that which for us may be confusing. The embodiments of God in every Word spoken to His servants are so important that it behooves those who are called of God with a deep sense of imperfection to search for and understand what is it that God is saying before any step is taken on His assignment. Too quickly, and too often, God's children are confused by the disastrous outcome of situations they have journeyed with, thinking that God was in on it from the beginning; only for them to discover they failed in asking God questions before embarking on the journey that they should not have began. Others in some situations stubbornly decided not to see beyond their own comfort of settlement 'what I have done was what God wanted,' therefore they say, I did what I did His way, without stopping to recall many times they chose to ignore the warning signs from God.

In the process of writing *I Hear You!...But What is God Saying?* I determined that God would lead me as in my last book for the work that will bring Him glory. It is on this very gratifying notion that the LORD has scripted the thoughts to His people through the pages uncovered here. God in His principles has never changed but humanity changes. The ways and methods of God from the generations past have remained the same. And it is on this premise that we as people must look back to the way God worked with those before us through Scripture, arbitrated through tradition. While our personal and social experiences with important reasoning are employed giving us the clear understanding of what it means to serve in the community called church. God must be the central focus of obedience which is the enablement that fulfills the duties of the work to which we are called in every step we take. Holiness in every sensibility must be encased in the essence of our worship to God without which we cannot please Him.

The goodness of God has never failed. The Grace and the Mercies of God will forever be greater than we can envision. When all is said and done, what is humankind, and what is within mankind without God? God is not only Lord over the entire world and its history, but in His eternal power and will God in every way continues to rule in the affairs of humanity according to His plan. As none of us can tell what the future holds we should and must be bowed on a bended knee seeking for the guidance of the One who holds the key to that path whose cave cannot be earthed until He unearths it.

Many times the embroidery of our understanding of God is seen through our limited worldview and life experience rather than through the Holy Spirit who allows for our true knowledge of Him. It takes the Holy Spirit to reveal to us a glimpse of the Mighty and Awesome God - the Creator of the universe. We as people must come to God with a surrendered heart knowing that we are nothing without Him; it is with this grateful heart of humility that we can change the world around us and beyond, by the leading of no more, no less, but the Holy Spirit.

I hear you! But what is God Saying? Has been written for the purpose of understanding that the God who calls us always welcomes our questions, and that once He has answered we have the choice to be obedient unto blessings, or to revel in rebellion.

May your lives richly be blessed, entered in His glory for ever and ever; Amen.